Solaris Essential Reference

New Riders

Other Titles by New Riders

Solaris Essential Reference

John P. Mulligan

New
Riders

201 West 103rd Street, Indianapolis, IN 46290

Solaris Essential Reference

Copyright © 1999 by New Riders Publishing

International Standard Book Number: 0-7357-0023-0

Library of Congress Catalog Card Number: 98-89434

Printed in the United States of America

First Printing: April, 1999

03 02 01 00 99   7 6 5 4 3 2 1

Interpretation of the printing code: The rightmost double-digit number is the year of the book's printing; the rightmost single-digit number is the number of the book's printing. For example, the printing code 99-1 shows that the first printing of the book occurred in 1999.

Trademarks

Warning and Disclaimer

Executive Editor
Laurie Petrycki

Acquisitions Editor
Katie Purdum

Development Editor
Jim Chalex

Managing Editor
Sarah Kearns

Project Editor
Jennifer Chisholm

Copy Editor
Daryl Kessler

Indexer
Lisa Stumpf

Technical Reviewers
Dean Neuman
Mary E. S. Morris

Proofreader
Megan Wade

Layout Technician
Cheryl Lynch

I would like to dedicate this book to Phil Kostenbader.
Thanks, Phil, for being a great boss, mentor, and friend.

About the Author

John P. Mulligan is the creator of the *Unofficial Guide to Solaris* (sun.icsnet.com), a popular Web site for users of the Solaris operating system. John spent three years in the Computing Support Services department at Lafayette College working on just about every aspect of UNIX systems administration and management. He was responsible for migrating all the college Sun SPARCstations from SunOS 4.x to Sun OS 5.x (a.k.a. Solaris 2). During that time, John also worked on a research project involving the modeling of microfluidic flows on Sun Solaris workstations. John currently lives in Spring Grove, Pennsylvania, and works at P. H. Glatfelter Company as an environmental engineer. He can be reached at solref@hotmail.com.

About the Technical Reviewers

Dean Neumann is a Certified Master C Programmer, Master UNIX Programmer, and Master UNIX System Administrator. He currently serves as Principal Consultant with Neumann and Associates Information Systems, Inc., where he provides POSIX systems design and development services and software process improvement consulting. Prior to this, Dean served as Vice President, Engineering, with TeleLink Technologies and as Director of Engineering with TGI Technologies. His graduate research was in the fields of synthetic holography and three-dimensional medical imaging, and his current interests include distributed and high availability systems, RDBMS and OODBMS systems, and Quality Management Systems. Mr. Neumann is a member of the IEEE and the IEEE Computer Society.

Mary E. S. Morris's work in the UNIX world includes more than a dozen flavors, but her favorites remain Solaris and Linux. Her tenure in the field includes consulting at several Fortune 1000 companies after building her UNIX foundation at Sun Microsystems as a system administrator, technical Webmaster, instructional designer, and consultant. She has also authored books (about Solaris, Web design and development, and careers for the cyber-professional) and teaches online at ZDU.

Contents

Part III Appendices

Acknowledgments

First, I want to thank my parents—my dad for giving me a love of science and technology, and my mom for giving me the writing skills to be able to put my thoughts into words. Mom and Dad, you have always been there for me, supporting me in everything I have ever done. I can never thank you enough. I also need to thank my brother Eddie, who is always there for me when I just need to have a long conversation about computers, technology, and other geeky things that no one else wants to hear about.

Thanks also go to everyone I worked with at New Riders— Laurie Petrycki, Jim Chalex, and Katie Purdum. They helped me turn my ideas into an actual book while displaying amazing amounts of patience. You all deserve a raise after working with me! I also thank the reviewers, Dean Neumann and Mary Morris, who helped to check my technical information.

There are many other people that I need to thank as well. Thanks Jaime, for everything—being excited for me, listening to me, laughing with me, sometimes humoring me, and always keeping me humble. Thanks Uncle Jimmy, for giving me the motivation to write something as large as a reference book and sharing your writing experience with me along the way. Thanks Aunt Mary, for just being my Aunt Mary. Thanks also go to Jamie, Jeff, and Tony at PHG; Gripp and Babump at Lafayette; and my fellow Lehightonians: Mo and Maia. And to everyone else who in some way supported my efforts—thank you.

Tell Us What You Think!

As the reader of this book, *you* are our most important critic and commentator. We value your opinion and want to know what we're doing right, what we could do better, what areas you'd like to see us publish in, and any other words of wisdom you're willing to pass our way.

As the Executive Editor for the *UNIX* team at New Riders specializing in all versions of *UNIX*, I welcome your comments. You can fax, email, or write me directly to let me know what you did or didn't like about this book—as well as what we can do to make our books stronger.

Please note that I cannot help you with technical problems related to the topic of this book, and that due to the high volume of mail I receive, I might not be able to reply to every message.

When you write, please be sure to include this book's title and author, as well as your name and phone or fax number. I will carefully review your comments and share them with the author and editors who worked on the book.

Fax: 317-581-4663

Email: newriders@mcp.com

Mail: Laurie Petrycki
          Executive Editor
          New Riders Publishing
          201 West 103rd Street
          Indianapolis, IN 46290 USA

Introduction

This book is designed to be the ideal reference for Solaris users who know what they want to do—but just need to know how to do it. This reference assumes that the reader is well versed in general UNIX skills and is simply in need of some pointers on how to get the most out of Solaris. Rather than a lengthy tutorial that holds the user's hand, this book serves as a desktop reference of everything an experienced user will need to know to use Solaris.

Although there are many versions of Solaris, this reference is concerned for the most part with Solaris 2.5 and 2.6—two of the most recent and widely used versions of Solaris. During the writing of this book, Solaris 2.7 (marketed under the name Solaris 7) was released. It includes a fully 64-bit operating system (SunOS 5.7) and many other enhancements. Although Solaris 7 is, in many ways, different from previous releases, everything in this reference will work on Solaris 7 as well. The new features of Solaris 7—many of which are graphical interfaces—are not covered in this text. However, a brief list of the new features has been included in Appendix A, "Solaris Version Changes."

I have placed the emphasis on the essentials of using the SunOS 5 operating system, rather than on using the OpenWindow environment. The general rule is that anything that can be done from a graphical user interface in Solaris can also be done from the command line. Using the command-line interface rather than a GUI allows users and administrators to have full access to Solaris computers even when they are not using a terminal that can support graphics. Therefore, the commands and explanations in this reference can be used via remote logins over corporate LANs, across the Internet, or while sitting at the actual computer console—regardless of what type of monitor or frame buffer is present.

Book Conventions

This book has been designed to facilitate quick searches. The best way you can speed up your searches is to understand the layout of this book. The following example can help you do this.

The first page of most chapters will have two *jump-tables*. The table on the left is a list of all the specific commands, utilities, and so on, that are featured in the chapter, in alphabetical order, with respective page numbers. The right jump-table reflects the order of the chapter as it actually appears. Each line in bold indicates the "highest" or "broadest" header. The following is an example of this level of chapter header.

Informational Utilities

The specific commands, tasks, utilities, and so forth, are listed in smaller headers, as follows.

finger

Following these smaller headers will be a consistent flow of information found throughout the book, including the syntax, description, options, commands, special elements and/or information, and relevant cross references.

```
/usr/bin/finger [options] {user}
```

The Description of finger.

Option	Description
-b	Do not show home directories and shells in the information given.
-z	Not an actual option. This is simply to display that information is listed in alphabetical order, if it is deemed useful to present it this way.

In-Depth Information or Special Warnings
These elements can be skipped, but usually include useful, extra information.

▶ **See Also** command (xxx)

There are also several typographical conventions that are used in this book. They are as follows:

Convention	Description	Example
Commands and scripts	Solaris commands, command lines, and shell scripts are shown in a monospaced font.	`/usr/ucb/ps -auxw ¦ grep inetd`
Variables	Variables that hold the place for substitutions are shown in italic and a monospaced font.	`cat` *`filename`*
Optional syntax	Optional items in a command's syntax appear in brackets.	`finger [`*`options`*`] [`*`host`*`]`
Keystrokes	Keystrokes and keystroke combinations appear in bold.	**CTRL+Z**

I

General Usage Reference

1
Text Utilities

Sorting

sort

sort

```
/usr/bin/sort [options] [files]
/usr/xpg4/bin/sort [options] [files]
```

Sort, reorder, and list the lines of a text file or stream. Temporary files are written to /var/tmp/stm*.

Option	Description
+n.m	If only n (an integer) is given, skip n fields before sorting. If n.m (both integers) is given, start at character n of the mth field.
-b	Ignore blanks, spaces, and tabs.
-c	Produce output only if the file is not already sorted. The xpg4 version produces no output under any circumstances.
-d	Use only letters, digits, and spaces for sorting. All other characters are ignored (dictionary sort).
-f	Case-insensitive sort. Ignore difference between upper and lowercase characters (folding).
-i	Ignore non-printable ASCII characters.
-k keydef	Restricted key sorting. Sorting is restricted to a portion of the line.
-m	Assume the file is already sorted and merge them.
-M	Sort as months using the first three non-blank characters (-b is implied).
-n	Sort by number (arithmetic value). Leading zeros are ignored.
-o file	Redirect the output to a file—either new or the input file itself.
-r	Reverse the sort.
-t char	Redefine the delimiter to char. The delimiters are spaces and tabs by default.
-T directory	Define temporary file directory. Use /var/tmp by default if not specified.
-u	Non-unique (repeated) lines appear only once.

continues >>

Option	Description
-y *kmem*	Set the amount of main memory to be used by sort. If -y is given without an amount (*kmem*), the maximum amount of memory is used.

Example	Task
sort -b userlist > userlist.sorted	Sort a list of usernames, ignoring leading spaces and tabs, outputting to a file.
repquota -a ¦ sort +2n	Sort the output of a quota report by disk usage.
sort hostlog ¦ uniq -c	Sort a list of hostnames, removing duplicates, and count the frequency of each one.

▶ **See Also** join (7), uniq (5)

uniq

usr/bin/uniq [*options*] [*files*]   uniq

Find, count, and delete repeated lines in text files or streams. If the repeated lines are not adjacent, they will not be detected. Therefore, it is recommended that the text be sorted first.

Option	Description
-c	Frequency count of each line.
-d	Do not output unique lines.
-f *fields*	Ignore the first *fields* fields when comparing lines. Also, -*fields* can be used with the same effect.
-s *chars*	Ignore the first *chars* characters when comparing lines. Also, +*chars* can be used with the same effect.
-u	Do not output non-unique lines.

Example	Task
last ¦ awk '{print $1}' ➡¦ sort ¦ uniq -c	Determine how many times users have logged in.
sort hostlog ¦ uniq ➡-c ¦ sort -rn	Sort hosts in a log file by frequency in decreasing order.
uniq -c datafile	Perform a simple frequency count of data.

▶ **See Also** sort (4)

Formatting

cut

cut   `/usr/bin/cut [options] [files]`

Select columns or fields out of a file. Either -b, -c, or -f must be used. Works well when used with paste.

Option	Description
-b *list*	Specify columns by byte size.
-c *list*	Specify columns by character positions.
-d *delim*	Use the character following -d as the delimiter. Spaces must be in quotes.
-f *list*	Specify what fields to cut using delimiter defined by -d.
-n	Do not split characters.
-s	Do not output lines that do not contain the delimiter specified with -d.

Example	Task
cut -c2	Show only the second column of a file.
cut -d: -f1,6/ ➡etc/passwd	Display usernames and their home directories.
cut -d" " ➡-f2 file	Show second column of a space delimited file.

▶ **See Also** awk (19), paste (10), join (7), newform (8)

fmt

fmt   `/usr/bin/fmt [options] [files]`

Generic text formatting utility to create lines of the same length. Blank lines and spacing are not altered during the formatting.

Option	Description
-c	Align the left margins of a paragraph with the line after the initial indentation.

continues >>

Option	Description
-s	Do not join lines. Useful when formatting code and formatted text.
-w *width*	Fill lines to *width*.

Example

```
cat myfile ¦ fmt -c
➡> alignedfile.txt
```

Task

Align the left margins of a text.

```
cat myfile ¦ fmt -w
➡> filledtext.txt
```

Fill lines of text to 80 columns.

▶ **See Also** newform (8)

fold

/usr/bin/fold [*options*] [*files*]   fold

This utility can be used to fold lines. This is done by inserting newline characters at a specified place in each line. Words will not be broken if a text file is folded.

Option	Description
-b	Measure the width in bytes.
-s	Break lines at blank characters.
-w *width*	Specifies maximum line width in characters. Default is 80.

Example

```
fold -b 32 myfile.txt
```

Task

Fold a text file to 32 bytes.

```
fold -s myfile.txt
➡> myfile2.txt
```

Insert newline characters into the text where there are blank characters; send the output to a new file.

▶ **See Also** cut (6), fmt (6), paste (10)

join

/usr/bin/join [*options*] [*files*]   join

A relational command that can be used to join two files.

Option	Description
-1 *field*	Join on the specified field of file 1.
-2 *field*	Join on the specified field of file 2.
-a *number*	Output a line for each unpairable line in the file specified by the number.
-e *string*	Replace blank output with the specified string.
-j *field*	Same as -1 *field* -2 *field*.
-j1 *field*	Same as -1 *field*.
-j2 *field*	Same as -2 *field*.
-o *list*	Output lines contain the fields specified in the list. If the fields specified in the list are not in the input, they will be treated as blank fields.
-t *char*	Use the specified character as the separator.
-v *filenumber*	Output only unpairable lines in the specified file.

▶ **See Also** awk (19), sort (4), uniq (5), cut (6), paste (10)

newform

newform   /usr/bin/newform [*options*] [*files*]

Utility to reformat text in a variety of ways, reading from files or from standard input. Note that command line options are processed in the order given. Similar to cut and paste.

Option	Description
-a *n*	Append *n* characters to the end of each line to obtain the line length specified by -l.
-b *n*	Trim *n* characters from the beginning of each line. If no *n* is given, the lines will be truncated to the effective line length.
-c *char*	Change the character used by -a or -p to *char*.
-e *n*	Trim *n* characters from the end of each line.
-f	Show the tab specification used by -o.
-i *spec*	Replace tabs with spaces using the given tab specification. (Opposite of -o)

continues >>

Option	Description
-1 *n*	Set the effective line length to *n* characters. Default is 72 if no value is given.
-o *tabspec*	Replace spaces with tabs using the given tab specification. (Opposite of -i)
-p *n*	Prepend *n* characters to the beginning of each line to obtain the length specified by -l.
-s	Remove leading character from each line up to the first tab, moving the first eight characters to the end of the line. Characters beyond the first eight are replaced by *.

▶ **See Also** fmt (6)

nl

```
/usr/bin/nl [options] [files]
/usr/xpg4/bin/nl [options] [files]
```
nl

Add line numbers to text either from a file or from standard input. Line numbers are added to the left side of the text, and reset at the top of each page.

Option	Description
-b *type*	Page numbering specification, which can be one of the following: ■ a: number all lines ■ n: no line numbers ■ t: number all non-empty lines ■ p *exp*: number only lines matching regular expression *exp*.
-d *chars*	Specify the two-character delimiter to be used for logical page breaks. If only one character is entered, the second is assumed to be a colon.
-f *type*	Page numbering specification for footer. Types are the same as -b.
-h *type*	Page numbering specification for header. Types are the same as -f and -b.
-i *n*	Increment page numbers by *n*.

continues >>

>>continued

Option	Description
-l *n*	Number of consecutive blank lines to count as a single line.
-n *format*	Line numbering format:
	■ ln: left justified, no leading zeros
	■ rn: right justified, no leading zeros
	■ rz: right justified
	Default is right justified with no leading zeros (rn).
-p	Do not reset page numbering at page breaks.
-s *sep*	Separating character between the line number and the text. By default the separator is a tab.
-v *n*	Starting page number.
-w *n*	Width of page numbers. Default is **6**.

Example	Task
nl source.c	Add line numbers to a source code file.
ls ¦ nl	Add line numbers to a directory listing.

▶ **See Also** sort (4), uniq (5), fmt (6)

paste

paste   /usr/bin/paste [*options*] [*files*]

The **paste** command joins specific lines of text contained in two files. This is done by replacing the newline character at the end of each line in the first file with a tab. The newline characters at the end of each line in the second file are not changed.

Option	Description
-d *delims*	The -d option is used to specify alternate delimiters for use when pasting two files. Delimiters are given in a list (with no spaces) in place of *delims*. Tabs can be specified as \t, and newline characters can be specified as \n.

Example	Task
paste *file1* *file2*	Join two corresponding lines in two files.

▶ **See Also** awk (19), cut (6), join (7), newform (8)

Editors

ed

```
/usr/bin/ed                                                          ed
/usr/bin/red
/usr/xpg4/bin
```

Command line-based text editor for UNIX operating systems. The `red` command is the restricted version of `ed`. Using `red` allows the user to edit only those files in the current directory, and the use of shell commands (!) is prohibited.

When executing shell commands, `/usr/bin/ed` uses `/usr/bin/sh` as the command interpreter. `/usr/xpg4/bin/ed` uses a `ksh`-compliant shell.

Commands

Commands are of the following form unless otherwise noted:

```
[address][command]
```

Command	Description
! *command* -*line*	The given command line is sent to the command shell and executed. The character ! will be replaced by the current filename.
!!	Repeat the last executed shell command.
a *text*	Append *text* after the addressed line.
addr	Output the specified address (*addr*) to standard output.
c *text*	Delete the addressed line and replace it with *text*.
d	Delete the addressed line(s).
e *file*	Empty the buffer and load *file* info into the buffer. The current line is set to the last line of the file. `ed` will first check to see if the current file has been saved since the last changes.
E *file*	Same as e *file*, except that no check is made to see if the current file has been saved since the last change.
f *file*	Change the current filename in use to *file*, regardless of whether *file* exists. All subsequent changes will be written to *file*.

continues >>

>>continued

Command	Description
G/*regexpr*/	Similar to the g command. Each line that matches the regular expression *regexpr* is displayed and a single command can be entered. That command is then executed on the displayed line. (Known as the *interactive global command*.)
g/*regexpr* /*command*	Execute *command* on every line in the buffer matching the regular expression specified by *regexpr*. (Known as the *global command*.)
h	Help. Displays a short message to explain the most recent diagnostic.
H	Help mode. All subsequent diagnostics produce error messages.
i *text*	Insert *text* before the addressed line.
j	Join lines between the two specified addresses. Newline characters are removed.
k*char*	Mark the addressed line with the character specified by *char*.
l	Write the addressed lines to standard output, showing all control characters and non-printable characters.
m*addr*	Move the addressed line to the address specified by *addr*.
n	Display the addressed lines with line numbers shown.
newline	Output the next line in the buffer to standard output.
p	Output the addressed lines to standard output.
P	Toggle prompting. If prompting is on, an asterisk is given on the line when waiting for a command. No addresses are required for this command.
q	Quit. If changes have been made since the last time the buffer has been saved, a warning is given.
Q	Quit without checking for unsaved changes.
r *file*	Read *file* into the current buffer without changing the current filename.
s/*regexpr*/ *text*/	Search the buffer for text matching the regular expression specified by *regexpr* and replace the first occurrence with *text*.
s/*regexpr*/ *text*/g	Similar to s/*regexpr*/*text*/, but replaces all occurrences.

continues >>

Command	Description
s/*regexpr*/ *text*/l	Similar to s/*regexpr*/*text*/, but outputs to standard output the last line in which the replacement was made.
s/*regexpr*/ *text*/*n*	Similar to s/*regexpr*/*text*/, but only replaces the nth occurrence.
s/*regexpr*/ *text*/*n*	Similar to s/*regexpr*/*text*/l, but outputs the last line in which a substitution was made in the format specified by *n*.
s/*regexpr*/ *text*/p	Similar to s/*regexpr*/*text*/l, but outputs the first line in which the substitution was made.
t*addr*	Same as the move command (m). However the addressed lines are copied after the address specified by *addr*.
u	Undo the last change made to the buffer.
v/*regexpr*/ *command*	Run *command* on all lines not matching the regular expression specified by *regexpr*.
w *file*	Write the addressed lines to the file specified by *file*. The file is created (mode 666) if it does not already exist.
W *file*	Append the addressed lines to the files specified by *file*. The file is created (mode 666) if it does not already exist.
X *key*	Toggle encryption on or off. Encryption will be performed using the key specified by *key*. If a key is not given, encryption will be turned off.

LIMITS

- 512 characters per line

- 256 characters in a command line (excluding ! commands)

- 255 characters in a pathname and/or filename (including slashes)

vi

```
/usr/bin/vi [options] [files]
/usr/bin/view [options] [files]
/usr/bin/vedit [options] [files]
/usr/xpg4/bin/vi [options] [files]
/usr/xpg/bin/view [options] [files]
/usr/xpg/bin/vedit [options] [files]
```

Edit and reformat text using a full-screen editor (visual editor), based on the ex editor. Using view instead of vi will cause the text file to be opened in read-only mode.

Option	Description
+command	Execute command when vi is started.
-c	Encryption mode. Same as -x, except that all text read is assumed to be encrypted.
-l	Configure vi to edit LISP programs.
-L	Report all saved files after vi was improperly shut down (editor crash, or system crash).
-R	Read-only mode.
-r filename	Recover a file left in the buffer after a system crash.
-s	Run in non-interactive mode (suppress feedback). This mode should be used when running non-interactive scripts.
-t tag	Edit the file that contains tag, and position the editor at its definition.
-v	Use vi in the display editing state.
-V	Verbose mode, sending output to standard error. Useful for debugging scripts when used in conjunction with -s.
-w n	Set the default window size to n characters wide.
-x	Encryption mode. The user is prompted for a key that will be used for encryption and decryption. Temporary buffers are encrypted as well.

Modes

	How to Enter Mode	How to Terminate Mode	Description
Command Mode	Start vi or exit other mode	q	This is the normal mode for vi, and the mode that is entered upon starting the editor. When other modes are finished or exited, vi returns to Command Mode. Pressing **ESC** will cancel a command before it is executed.
Input Mode	A, I, O, C, S, (upper or lower case), or R	ESC	Text may be entered in this mode.

Canceling Commands

Keystroke	Effect
ESC	Terminate input mode or cancel a command before it is executed.
DEL	Interrupt.

File Manipulation

Command	Description
ZZ	If the current file has been changed; save and exit. Otherwise, just exit.
:w	Save changes. (Write-out.)
:q	Quit without saving changes.
:e *file*	Edit *file*.
:e!	Reopen file for editing, discarding any previous changes.
:w *file*	Save *file*.
:w! *file*	Save *file*, overwriting if it already exists.
:sh	Start shell, and then return to vi when done.
:! *command*	Run *command* and return to vi.
:n	Specify new argument list.
^G	Report the current filename and line.
:ta *tag*	Position cursor to the *tag*.

Movement and Positioning

Command	Description
^F	Forward one screen.
^B	Back one screen.
^U	Scroll up half screen.
^D	Scroll down half screen.
*n*G	Go to the beginning of line number *n*.
/*pattern*	Go to the next occurrence matching the specified *pattern*.

continues >>

>>continued

Command	Description
?pattern	Go to the last occurrence matching the specified *pattern*.
N	Repeat the last ? or / search.
N	Reverse the last / or ? search.
/pattern/+n	Go to the nth line after the specified pattern.
?pattern?-n	Go to the nth line before the specified pattern.
]]	Next section.
[[	Previous section.
(	Go to the beginning of the current sentence.
)	Go to the end of the current sentence.
{	Go to the beginning of the paragraph.
}	Go to the end of the paragraph.
%	Find pairs of brackets or parentheses.
H	Go to the top (head) of the screen.
L	Go to the bottom (last line) of the screen.
M	Go to the middle of the screen.
+	Next line.
-	Previous line.
Carriage return	Same as +.
v or j	Next line but stay in the same column.
^ or k	Previous line but stay in the same column.
^	Go to the first non-blank character.
0	Beginning of line.
$	End of line.
:$	Go to the end of the file.
l, **Space** →	Forward one character.
h, **CTRL+H** ←	Back one character.
F*x*	Find next occurrence of *x*.
F*x*	Find previous *x*.
T*x*	Move to the character just before the next *x*.

continues >>

Command	Description
T*x*	Move to the character directly following *x*.
;	Repeat the last f, F, t, or T command issued.
,	Repeat the inverse of the last f, F, t, or T command issued.
n¦	Move to column *n*.
w	Forward one word.
b	Back one word.
e	Go to the end of the word.
W	Forward one blank-delimited word.
B	Back one blank-delimited word.
e	Go to the last character of a blank-delimited word.

Marking Text

Command	Description
M*x*	Mark current position (with an *x*).
`*x*	Go to next mark.
'*x*	Move cursor to first character (non-space) in the marked line.

Inserting and Replacing Text

Command	Description
^H	Delete previous character (**Backspace**).
^W	Delete the previous word.
ERASE CHARACTER	Same as **Backspace**.
KILL CHARACTER	Delete current line.
\	Display the current kill and erase characters.
^D	Backtab one character and reset left margin.
CONTROL+D	Backtab to beginning of line without resetting left margin.
0^D	Backtab to the beginning of the line and reset the left margin.
^V	Quote a non-printable character.

continues >>

>>continued

Command	Description
a	Append text after the current position.
A	Append text at the end of the current line.
II	Insert text before current position.
I	Insert text before the first non-blank character.
R*char*	Replace a single character with the specified character, *char*.
R*chars*ESC	Replace multiple characters specified by *chars*.

Operators

vi also can be controlled using operators. To use any of the following operators, type the given operator followed by a cursor movement. The following example will "yank" the subsequent sentence to the buffer:

    y)

Operator	Action
!	Filter the text through a command.
<	Shift left.
>	Shift right.
c	Change.
C	Change an entire line of text.
d	Delete.
D	Delete an entire line of text.
J	Join lines.
s	Substitute characters.
S	Substitute whole lines.
U	Undo last change.
x	Delete characters.
X	Delete characters before current position.
y	Copy to buffer (also called *yanking*).
Y	Copy lines (*yank*).
p	Put yanked lines before current position.
P	Put yanked lines after current position.

▶ **See Also** ed (11), sed (31), awk (19)

Advanced Text Tools

awk

    /usr/bin/awk [*options*] [*files*]   awk

A text utility that uses a scripting language.

Option	Description
-f *file*	Use *file* as the program file to use.
-F*char*	Use *char* as the field separator.

Pre-Defined Variables

Variable	Description
FILENAME	Current filename.
FS	Current field separator. Can be changed on the command line with -F.
NF	Number of fields in the current record.
NR	Number of the current record.
OFMT	Number format. Default is %.6g.
OFS	Field separator to use for output. Default is blank.
ORS	Field separator to use for records. Default is newline.
RS	Input record field separator. Default is newline.

Actions and Functions

Action/ Function	Description
Break	Break out of a loop.
Continue	Go directly to the next iteration of a loop.
Exit	Stop reading input and exit.
exp(*x*)	Return the value of e^x.

continues >>

>>continued

Action/ Function	Description
for(*expr1*; *expr2*; *expr3*) *command*	Three expressions control the for loop: ■ *expr1* initializes the loop. ■ *expr2* is the test case. ■ *expr3* is used to change the loop variable. For example, to increment a variable to a certain number: `for(i=0; i<10; i++)` *command* Also, to run a command for each record in an array: `for` (*record* `in` *array*) *command*
Getline	Read the next record from the current input file.
index(*string1*, *string2*)	Give the position of *string1* in *string2*. Zero is returned if *string1* is not found.
int(*n*)	Convert *n* to an integer by truncation.
length(*string*)	Return the length of string.
match(*string*, *egexpr*)	Give the position of the regular expression *regexpr* in the given string.
next	Go to the next line of input.
print	Print the arguments to standard output. To print fields (separated by the field separator FS) use $*fieldnumber* (for example, `print $3` would print the third field). Redirection and pipes can be used with print statements.
printf	Same as print, but uses C `printf` formatting. Valid formats include the following: ■ Decimal number: %d ■ Strings: %s ■ Floating Point Numbers: %*x*.*y*f (in which *x* is the total number of digits, and *y* is the number of digits after the decimal point).
split(*string*, *a*,*fs*)	Split *string* into an array specified by *a* using *fs* as the field separator. The array has elements of *a*[1], *a*[2] … *a*[*n*].

continues >>

Action/ Function	Description
sprintf (*format*, *expr*, *expr*)	Format the expressions in a similar manner to printf.
substr (*string*,*m*,*n*)	Return the first *n* characters of *string*, that begin at position *m*.

▶ **See Also** sed (31), ed (11), vi (13)

ex

```
/usr/bin/ex [options] [files]
/usr/xpg4/bin/ex [options] [files]
```
ex

Text editor based on the ed editor and related to the vi editor.

Option	Description
+*command*	Same as -c *command*.
-C	Same as the x option, but all text read is assumed to be encrypted.
-c *command*	Execute *command* upon startup.
-l	Use LISP mode for editing.
-L	Display the names of all files saved after the editor was improperly exited.
-R	Read only mode. No changes are made to the file.
-r *file*	Recover and edit *file* that was left in the buffer after ex was improperly shut down.
-s	Do not output anything. Useful when used in scripts where no user feedback is required.
-v	Use in visual editing mode. Same as running vi.
-V	Verbose output.
-w*n*	Set the screen size to *n* characters wide.
-x	Encrypted mode. This option will prompt the user for an encryption key.

Mode	Description
Command	Normal state. ex starts up in this mode. A: is shown as a command prompt.
Insert	Type **a**, **c**, or **i** to enter Insert Mode. Enter a **.** on a line to exit to Command Mode.
Visual	Type **vi** to enter Visual Mode. Type **Q** to exit to Command Mode.

Commands

Task	Command	Description
Abbreviate	ab [*string1*] [*string2*]	After issuing this command, whenever *string1* is typed it is replaced with *string2*.
Adjust Window	[*addr*] z [*option*][*n*]	Print the lines starting at the addressed line and going *n* lines, in lines, in an adjusted window. Options are as follows: ■ -: Addressed line at bottom. ■ .: Addressed line at center. ■ +: Addressed line at top. ■ ^: Previous window. ■ =: Set current line to addressed line and place it at the center of the window.
Append	[*addr*] a[!] *text*	Insert *text* after the addressed lines. The use of ! will toggle autoindenting.
Arguments	*ar*	Display files that are being edited.
Change	[*addr*] c[!] *text*	Replace the addressed lines with *text*. The use of ! will toggle autoindenting.
Change Directory	cd *directory*	Change the current directory to *directory*.
Copy	[*addr1*] co [*addr2*]	Copy the text addressed by *addr1* to *addr2*.
Delete	[*addr*] d [*buffer*]	Delete the addressed text. If a buffer is specified, copy the deleted text to *buffer*.

continues >>

Task	Command	Description
Edit	e[!] [+*line*] [*file*]	Edit the file specified by *file* at line *line*. If ! is used, the current file is not saved before closing.
Encryption	X	Using encryption, attempt to determine if input is encrypted or not.
Escape	[*addr*] !*command*	Execute command on the addressed lines replacing them with the output. If no address is given the command simply runs and sends the output to standard output.
File	f [*file*]	If no filename is specified, just display the current file name. If a filename is specified, change the current filename to *file*.
Forced Encryption	C	Assume all input is encrypted text.
Global	[*addr*] g[!]/ *pattern*/ [*command*]	If lines are addressed, execute command on all addressed lines. If no lines are addressed, the command is run on lines matching the pattern. If no command is given, the lines are sent to standard output. ! reverses the matching pattern (commands are lines that do not match the pattern).
Insert	[*addr*] i[!] *text*	Insert text before the addressed lines. ! toggles autoindenting.
Join	[*addr*] j[!] [*count*][*flags*]	Join addressed lines into a single line, putting two spaces after a period. ! joins the lines without adding spaces.
List	[*addr*] l	List addressed lines, printing tabs (^I) and newlines ($).
Map	map[!] [*macro commands*]	Create a macro named *macro* that will perform the commands specified by *commands*.

continues >>

>>continued

Task	Command	Description
Mark	[addr] ma [mark]	Mark the addressed lines with the character mark.
Move	[addr1] m [addr2]	Move the lines addressed by addr1 to addr2.
Next	n[!] [files]	Begin editing the next file in the file list. If a file list is specified by files, the current file list is ignored. ! current changes are not saved.
Number	[addr] nu [n]	Display the addressed lines with line numbers. If a number n is given, n lines are shown starting with the addressed line.
Open	[addr] o [/pattern/]	vi mode is entered (single line vi commands can be used) starting at the text addressed by addr or matched by pattern.
Preserve	pre	Save the current file to the system save area.
Print	[addr] p [n]	Print n lines starting at the address specified by addr.
Print Next	<newline>	Print the next line to standard output.
Put	[addr] pu [buffer]	Put the contents of buffer at the address specified by addr.
Quit	q[!]	Quit. ! quits without saving any changes.
Read	[addr] r [file]	Insert the text from file after the addressed lines. A command can be used in place of a file by typing !command.
Recover	rec [file]	Recover file from system save area. Refer to Preserve, earlier in this table.
Rewind	rew[!]	Rewind to the first file in the file list. ! changes to the first file without saving changes.

continues >>

Task	Command	Description
Shell	sh	Use a new shell and edit after it exits.
Shell Escape	!	Go to shell.
Shift Left	[addr] < [n]	Shift addressed lines n characters left.
Shift Right	[addr] > [n]	Shift addressed lines n characters right.
Source	so script	Run an ex script specified by script.
Substitute	[addr] s [/pattern/ text/][opt] [n]	Substitute text matching pattern with text starting at the addressed line and going n lines. Options are as follows: ■ c: Confirm each substitution. ■ g: Global substitution. ■ p: Print the last line that was substituted.
Tag	ta tag	Begin editing the file that contains the tag specified by tag.
Unabbreviate	una string	Unabbreviate string. Refer to Abbreviate, earlier in this table.
Undo	u	Undo last change.
Unmap	unm[!] macro	Unmap the macro specified by the character macro. ! removes input mode macros.
Version	ve	Display ex current version number.
Visual	[address] vi [winsize]	Edit using visual mode starting at the addressed lines using a window size of winsize.
Write	[addr] w[!] [>>][file]	Write the addressed lines to file. If >> is used, the lines are appended to file. ! causes ex to overwrite the file.
Write and Quit	wq	Write and quit. ! ensures that none of the current contents of the current file are overwritten.
Yank	[addr] ya [buffer][n]	Yank n lines to buffer starting at the addressed lines. The general buffer is used if none is specified.

Editing Options

Task	Option	Description
Autoindent	Ai	Automatically indent lines.
Autowrite Directory	Aw	Always save changes before changing files.
Exrc	Ex	Read .exrc on startup.
Ignore Case	Ic	Ignore the case when doing pattern matching.
List	List	Display tabs (^I) and newlines ($).
Magic	magic	Treat ., [, and * as special characters in patterns.
Mode Lines	modelines	First and last five lines are executed as ex commands. They must be in one of the following forms: ■ ex:*command*: ■ vi:*command*:
Number	Nu	Show line numbers.
Paragraphs	Para	Use first character of each paragraph as a macro.
Redraw	Redraw	Attempt to use terminal as if it were a smart terminal.
Report	Report	If the last command modified more commands than the report variable, the user is notified.
Scroll	Scroll	Command mode lines.
Section	Sect	Section starting macros.
Show Mode	Smd	Show vi insert mode.
Slow Open	Slow	Do not update during inserts.
Terminal	term	Sets terminal type.
Window	window	Visual mode lines.
Wrap Margins	wm	Automatically wrap (split) lines at margins.

continues >>

Task	Option	Description
Wrap Searches	ws	Searches wrap when the end of the file is reached.

▶ **See Also** sed (31), ed (11), awk (19), vi (13)

grep

/usr/bin/grep [*options*] *pattern* [*file*]   grep

The grep text utility is used to find specific strings or patterns within a file. The default behavior of grep is to print all lines of text that match the given pattern or contain a specified string. The utility can also accept input from standard input if no file is specified.

Option	Description
-b	Print block numbers for each line.
-c	Print the number of lines that match the pattern.
-h	When searching multiple files, do not print the filename before each line.
-i	Perform a case-insensitive search.
-l	List the files in which the pattern is matched. If the pattern is found more than once in a file, the filename is printed only once.
-n	Show line numbers for each line printed.
-s	Do not show any error messages.
-v	Inverse. Print all lines that do not match the pattern.

Example	Task
grep smith /etc/passwd	Print all occurrences of the name smith in the system password file.
grep security *	Print the filenames and lines containing the word security in all files in the current directory.
/usr/ucb/ps -auxw ➡¦ grep smithj	Display all the processes currently owned by smithj.
grep -v false *file2*	Print all the lines that do not contain the word false in the file.

nawk

nawk   /usr/bin/nawk [*options*] ['*program*']
/usr/xpg4/bin/awk [*options*] ['*program*']

A text utility that uses a scripting language. nawk can do everything that awk can do, but more.

Option	Description
-f *file*	Uses *file* as the program file to use. If multiple -f options are used, the specified files are joined and used as a single program.
-F*char*	Use *char* as the field separator. A regular expression can also be used in place of *char*.

Pre-Defined Variables

Variable	Description
ARGC	Number of command line arguments.
ARGV ARGV[1] ...ARGV[ARGC]	Array of command line arguments.
CONVFMT	Number conversion format. Used for printf number converting only—not output statements.
FILENAME	Current filename.
FNR	Relative number of the current record.
FS	Current field separator. Can be changed on the command line with -F.
LENGTH	The length of the string matched by the match command.
NF	Number of fields in the current record.
NR	Number of the current record.
OFMT	Number format. Default is %.6g.
OFMT	Current number format. Default is %.6g.
OFS	Field separator to use for output. Default is blank.
ORS	Field separator to use for records. Default is newline.
RS	Input record field separator. Default is newline.
RSTART	The position of the first character in the string matched by the match function.
SUBSEP	Array subscript separator.

Actions and Functions

Action/ Function	Description
atan2(*x*,*y*)	Arctangent of *x*/*y*.
Break	Break out of a loop.
close(*expr*)	Close the file or pipe specified by *expr*.
Continue	Go directly to the next iteration of a loop.
cos(*x*)	Cosine of *x*.
Do *Statements* while(*expr*) (while(*expr*) *statement*)	Loop. Statements in the body of the loop (statements) are executed until the expression *expr* is true. The while command can also be used by itself.
Exit	Stop reading input and exit.
exp(*x*)	Return the value of e^x.
expr ¦ getline	The return value of *expr* is sent to getline.
for(*expr1*: *expr2*: *expr3*) *command*	Three expressions control the for loop: ■ *expr1* initializes the loop. ■ *expr2* is the test case. ■ *expr3* is used to change the loop variable. A common example is to increment a variable to a certain number: for(i=0; i<10; i++)*command*
for(*record* in *array*) *command*	Run *command* for each *record* in *array*.
function *fname*(*args*) {*statements*}	User-defined functions: ■ *fname* is the function name. ■ *args* are any arguments to be passed to the function. ■ *statements* are the function statements enclosed in braces.
Getline	Read the next record from the current input file.

continues >>

>>*continued*

Action/ Function	Description
getline < *expr*	Evaluate *expr* and treat the return value as a filename. The input is then taken from that filename.
getline *variable*	Assign the value of the next line of input to *variable*.
gsub(regexpr, *index* (*string1*, *string2*))	Give the position of *string1* in *string2*. Zero is returned if *string1* is not found.
int(*n*)	Convert *n* to an integer by truncation.
length(*string*)	Return the length of string.
log(*x*)	Natural log of *x*.
match(*string*, *regexpr*)	Give the position of the regular expression *regexpr* in the given *string*.
Next	Go to the next line of input.
print	Print the arguments to standard output. To print fields (separated by the field separator FS), use $*fieldnumber* (for example, print $3 would print the third field). Redirection and pipes can be used with print statements.
printf	Same as print, but uses C printf formatting. Valid formats include the following: ■ Decimal number: %*d* ■ Strings: %*s* ■ Floating Point Numbers: %*x*.*y*f (in which *x* is the total number of digits, and *y* is the number of digits after the decimal point)
rand()	Return a random number between 0 and 1.
sin(*x*)	Sine of *x*.
split(*string*, *a*,*fs*)	Split *string* into an array specified by *a* using *fs* as the field separator. The array has elements of *a*[1], *a*[2] ... *a*[*n*].
sprintf (*format*, *expr*,*expr*)	Format the expressions in a similar manner to printf.

continues >>

Action/ Function	Description
sqrt(*x*)	Square root of *x*.
srand(*n*)	Seed the random number generator (rand()) with *n*. If *n* is omitted, the time of day is used.
sub(*regexp*, *string*)	Replace the text that is matched by the regular expression with *string*.
substr (*string*,*m*,*n*)	Return the first *n* characters of *string*, that begin at position *m*.
system(*expr*)	Execute the command name returned by the evaluation of the expression specified by *expr*. Similar to the system() C function.
tolower (*string*)	Return *string* in all lowercase letters.
toupper (*string*)	Return *string* in all uppercase letters.

▶ **See Also** sed (31), ed (11), vi (13)

sed

```
/usr/bin/sed [option] [file]
/usr/xpg4/sed [options] [file]
```

sed

Text utility to edit/modify streams and files.

Option	Description
-e *command*	Run the edit command specified by *command*. More than one -e can be specified from the command line.
-f *file*	Take the editing commands from the script file specified by *file*.
-n	No output.

Edit Commands

Edit commands are very similar to the command–line usage of the ed editor. They take the following form:

```
[addresses] command [arguments]
```

Command	Description
! *command*	Run *command* on the lines *not* addressed.
#	Comment. If a # is the first character of any line, that line is treated as a comment and ignored. See #n.
#n	If a # directly followed by an *n* are the first two characters of any line, the output for the rest of the script will be suppressed.
:*label*	Assign a label called *label* for use in a script. By itself, this command does nothing.
{*commands*}	Execute *commands* on the addresses specified.
{*commands*}}	Execute *commands* on the selected pattern space.
=}	Print the current line number to standard output.
a *text*	Append *text* after each addressed line. Results are sent to standard output.
b *label*	Go directly to :*label* in the script. The command directly following :*label* is the next to be executed.
c *text*	Replace the addressed text with *text*.
d	Delete the addressed text.
D	Delete a multi-part pattern up to the first newline. Multi-part patterns are formed by using the N command.
g	Replace the pattern space with the hold space. The hold space is set by using the h or H command. Similar to pasting from a clipboard.
G	Similar to g, but the hold space is appended to the pattern rather than replacing it. Similar to pasting from a clipboard.
h	Copy the pattern space to the hold space. Similar to copying something to a clipboard. Previous contents of hold space are replaced.
H	Similar to h, but the pattern space is appended to the hold space, rather than replacing it.
i *text*	Insert *text* before each addressed line. Results are sent to standard output.

continues >>

Command	Description
L	Print the pattern space on standard output, including control characters and non-printable characters.
n	Replace the pattern space with the next line of text. Results are sent to standard output.
N	Similar to n, but the next line is appended to the pattern space rather than replacing it.
p	Print the pattern space to standard output up to the next newline.
P	Print the pattern space to standard output.
Q	Quit. If an address is given, the addressed line is sent to standard output before exiting.
r *file*	Append the contents of the file specified by *file* directly after the pattern space.
s/*regexp*/ *text*/	Substitute. Substitute the text for *flags* with the regular expression specified by *regexpr*. The following flags change the behavior of the substitution: ■ n: If an integer *n* is used, only the *n*th match will be substituted (*n*=1...512). ■ g: Global substitution. Substitute all matches. ■ p: Print the pattern space for substitutions made. ■ w *file*: If any substitutions are made they are written to file. Using w will erase the current contents of *file* if it already exists, and all substitutions will be appended to the file.
t *label*	If any changes have been made to the addressed lines, go to :*label* in the script.
w *file*	Write the pattern space to the file specified by file. The pattern space is appended to the end of the file.
X	Same as h. Exchange the pattern space and hold space contents.
y/*string1*/ *string2*	Transform the characters of two equal-length strings. *String1* must have the same number of characters as *string2*.

▶ **See Also** awk (19), nawk (28), ed (11), grep (27), ex (21)

2
Shell Scripting

Page	Contents

Shell Summary

Shell Name	Path	Startup Files
Bourne Shell (sh)	/sbin/sh	.profile

Built-in Commands bg, break, case, cd, chdir, continue, echo, eval, exec, exit, export, fg, for, getopts, hash, if, jobs, kill, login, logout, newgrp, pwd, read, readonly, return, set, shift, stop, suspend, test, times, trap, type, ulimit, umask, unset, until, wait, while

Standard Environment Variables HOME, PATH, CDPATH, MAIL, MAILCHECK, MAILPATH, PS1, PS2, IFS, SHACCT, SHELL, LC_CTYPE, LC_MESSAGES

Shell Name	Path	Startup Files
C Shell (csh)	/usr/bin/csh	.cshrc

Built-in Commands alias, bg, break, case, cd, chdir, continue, dirs, echo, eval, exec, exit, fg, foreach, glob, goto, hashstat, history, if, jobs, kill, limit, login, logout, nice, notify, onintr, popd, pushd, rehash, prepeat, set, setenv, shift, source, stop, suspend, switch, time, umask, unalias, unhash, unlimit, unset, unsetenv, wait, while

Standard Environment Variables ARGV, CDPATH, CWD, ECHO, FIGNORE, FILEC, HARDPATHS, HISTCHARS, HISTORY, HOME, IGNOREEOF, MAIL, NOBEEP, NOCLOBBER, NOGLOB, NONOMATCH, NOTIFY, PATH, PROMPT, SAVEHIST, SHELL, STATUS, TIME, VERBOSE

Shell Name	Path	Startup Files
Korn Shell (ksh)	/usr/bin/ksh	.profile

Built-in Commands alias, bg, break, case, cd, continue, echo, eval, exec, exit, export, fc, fg, for, function, getopts, hash, if, jobs, kill, let, login, logout, newgrp, print, pwd, read, readonly, return, select, set, shift, stop, suspend, test, times, trap, type, typeset, unlimit, umask, unalias, unset, until, wait, whence, while

Standard Environment Variables ERRNO, OLDPWD, OPTARG, OPTIND, PPID, PWD, RANDOM, REPLY, SECONDS, CDPATH, COLUMNS, EDITOR, ENV, FCEDIT, FPATH, IFS, HISTFILE, HISTSIZE, HOME, LC_ALL, LC_COLLATE, LC_CTYPE, LC_MESSAGES, LANG, LINENO, LINES, MAIL, MAILCHECK, MAILPATH, NLSPATH, PATH, PPID, PS1, PS2, PS3, PS4, SHELL, TMOUT, VISUAL

Executing Scripts and Commands

eval   sh csh ksh

eval   eval *argument*

The **eval** command reads the subsequent arguments into the shell and executes them as commands. This is useful for executing command lines that are generated by another program, such as another shell script.

▶ **See Also** exec (38), source (38)

exec   sh csh ksh

exec   exec *command* [*command arguments*]

The **exec** command is used to run a command without starting a new process. The new command will take the place of the current shell until it has terminated. Input and output from the command being executed may affect the current shell. Arguments can be sent to the command specifying them after the command name. The syntax of this command is the same for all the shells: sh, ksh, and csh.

▶ **See Also** eval (38), source (38)

source   csh

source   source [*options*] *filename*

The **source** command is available only in the csh shell. It reads the file specified and executes the commands. This command is useful for rereading a user's .cshrc file if something has been changed in it, such as a PATH.

Example	Task
source .cshrc	Update environment after changing the startup file.

▶ **See Also** exec (38), eval (38)

Setting and Unsetting Environment Variables

export   sh ksh

The set command does not necessarily make variables available for
subsequent commands to use. This is done by using the export command.
The export command sends the variable and its value to the shell environment, causing its value to be set and used by all other commands until
it is unset. The csh shell does not use the export command. It uses the
setenv command instead.

sh Syntax

    export [variable]

ksh Syntax

    export [variable [=value]]

Example	Task
export score1	Export the variable score1 using the sh shell.
export score1=100	Export the variable score1 and set it to 100 using the ksh shell.

▶ **See Also** set (39), unset (42), setenv (41), unsetenv (42)

set   sh csh ksh

The set command is one of the commands used to set environment
variables. In the case of the csh and ksh shells, the arguments of the set
command are variables that will be assigned the null value. Alternatively,
the csh command can also be used to assign a specific value to a variable
using an equal sign (=). For the sh shell, the environment values $1, $2, $3,
and so on are assigned the values of the first, second, and third arguments,
respectively. In all cases, if the set command is issued with no arguments,
the values of all environment variables are displayed.

sh Syntax

    set [options] [arguments]

Option	Description
—	Treat all options as arguments. (Necessary to set a variable to a dash.)
-a	Variables that are to be exported are noted.
-e	If an error is encountered (a non-zero exit status), exit immediately.
-f	Suppress filename generation.
-k	All keywords are treated as arguments, not just those after the command.
-n	Do not execute any commands.
-t	Read and execute only one command.
-u	If the variable is currently unset, return an error code.
-v	Verbose. Print all command lines when they are read.
-x	Verbose. Print all command lines when they are executed.

csh Syntax

```
set [variable [=variable]]
```

ksh Syntax

```
set [options] [arguments]
```

Option	Description
—	Ignore all other options.
-A	Treat the first argument as a variable name. Unset any previously assigned value and make the variable an array. The remaining arguments are assigned to each element of the array in order.
-a	Automatically export all variables.
-e	If an error is encountered (a non-zero exit status), exit.
-f	Suppress filename generation.
-k	All keywords are treated as arguments, not just those after the command.

continues >>

Option	Description
-m	Display a status message when background jobs are running and when they finish.
-n	Do not execute any commands. Command lines are checked for errors.
-t	Read and execute only one command.
-u	If the variable is currently unset, return an error code.
-v	Verbose. Print all shell command lines when they are executed.

Example	Task
set foo=2	Set the variable foo to the value of 2 using the csh shell.
set cat	Set the environment variable $1 to the value of cat using the sh shell.
set test1 test2	Clear the values of the variables test1 and test2.

▶ **See Also** unset (42), export (39), setenv (41), unsetenv (42)

setenv   csh

    setenv [*variable* [*value*]]   setenv

The setenv command is similar to the export command of the sh and csh shells. It sets and exports a variable to the shell environment. After the setenv command has been used on a variable, the variable and its value are available for use by all other subsequent commands. If no arguments are specified, all the currently set environment variables and their values will be displayed.

Example	Task
setenv	Show all environment variables and their values.
setenv PATH $PATH' ➡:/usr/sbin'	Add /usr/sbin to the current PATH variable in the csh shell.

▶ **See Also** set (39), unset (42), export (39), unsetenv (42)

unset   sh csh ksh

unset

The unset command is used to clear the value of environment variables. For the sh and ksh shells, the behavior is the same. The csh unset command works in a similar fashion but can also use wildcards (*) to do pattern matching. It should be noted that accidentally typing unset * in the csh shell will unset all environment variables and can cause problems.

sh Syntax

```
unset [variables]
```

csh Syntax

```
unset [variables]
```

ksh Syntax

```
unset [options] [variables]
```

Option	Description
-f	Unset the variable even if it is a function name, such as ERRNO or TMOUT.

Example	Task
unset test1 test2 test3	Unset three variables using the sh shell.
unset test1	Unset the variable called test1 using the csh shell.
unset -f ERRNO	Unset the ERRNO function variable using the ksh shell.
unset cat*	Unset all variables that begin with cat using the csh shell.

▶ **See Also** set (39), export (39), setenv (41), unsetenv (42)

unsetenv   csh

unsetenv

The unsetenv command is used to unset the environment variables in the csh shell. The command behaves much like the unset command of the sh and ksh shells.

csh Syntax

```
unsetenv variable
```

Example	Task
unsetenv TOPO	Unset the environment variable called TOPO.

▶ **See Also** set (39), unset (42), export (39), setenv (41)

RC File Environment Variable

HISTORY   csh

HISTORY specifies the number of lines to be stored in the command history. By default this is set to 1. The ksh shell uses the fc command to execute and edit previous commands.

HISTORY

Example	Description
set HISTORY=20	Set the history to 20 command lines.

LD_LIBRARY_PATH   sh csh ksh

LD_LIBRARY_PATH is the search path for dynamically linked libraries. Although this is not specific to any command shell, it is important in many cases. If a needed path is missing from this environment variable, an error similar to the following will be returned upon executing a command:

LD_LIBRARY _PATH

```
fatal: libfoo.s.o2: can't open file: errno=2
```

To fix this problem, find the path of the necessary library (for example, libfoo.so.2) and add that path to LD_LIBRARY_PATH.

Example	Description
set LD_LIBRARY_PATH=/usr/ ➡X11R6.1/lib:/usr/dt/lib	Set the dynamically loading library path.

EDITOR   sh csh ksh

Defines what editor to use when called by certain programs. For example, crontab will use the editor defined in EDITOR to edit the crontab file.

EDITOR

Example	Description
set EDITOR=/usr/ ➡local/bin/pico	Set the default editor to pico.

IFS   sh ksh

IFS

IFS specifies the internal field separator for the shell. The IFS character is used as the delimeter to interpret command lines. More than one character can be specified. IFS is set to SPACE, TAB, and NEWLINE by default. This can be useful when parsing text files. For example, when parsing the password file, it is useful to set the IFS to a colon (:).

Example	Description
set IFS=':'	Set the internal field separator to a colon.

PATH   sh csh ksh

PATH

PATH defines the search path for commands. If a command line begins with /, it is taken to be a fully qualified path name and PATH is ignored. Otherwise, the paths specified are searched in order until the command is found. If no matching command is found in the PATH, an error is returned. A dot (.) in the path causes the current working directory to be included in the path. For security reasons the dot (if included) should always be last in the path list.

Example	Description
set PATH=/usr/bin:/usr/ ➥ucb:/usr/ local/bin:.	Set a simple user PATH variable.

PROMPT   csh

PROMPT

Sets the prompt used for command lines. By default, this is set to %.

Example	Description
set PROMPT="'hostname':"	Use a prompt that displays the current hostname and the current shell level.

Input and Output

Command-Line Arguments

Command-
Line
Arguments

It is possible to use command-line arguments when writing shell scripts. This is done by using $1, $2, $3, and so on, in the script. The script name, as executed, is $0. The first argument is $1, and so on.

Example

```
Consider the following command line:
In this case the arguments are as follows:
$0 = myscript
$1 = apple
$2 = cow
$3 = monkey
```

Suppose a line in the script reads as follows:

```
echo "The second argument is $2."
```

As a result, the following line will print:

```
The second argument is cow.
```

echo   sh csh ksh

Print text to standard output. By default, the text is terminated with a   echo
newline when displayed.

Option	Description
-n	Suppress newlines. A newline is not added to the end of output.

Example	Description
`echo -n "Waiting 10 seconds..." sleep 10 echo "done."`	Print the first line, wait 10 seconds, and then print "done" on the same line.

read   sh ksh

Read from standard input and assign to variables.   read

ksh Options

Option	Description
-p	Take input from the output of a coprocess.
-r	Raw. Do not allow newlines to be escaped to continue lines (e.g. adding \ at the end of a line).
-s	Save. Input read is saved to the command history.
-u *descrip*	Input is read from the file descriptor specified by *descrip*.

Example	Description
read *id contents capacity*	Assign the first field (delimited by IFS) to $id, the second to $contents, and the third to $capacity.

Redirection

¦
¦

¦   Action: Pipe. Sends the standard output of one command or script to another command.

Example	Description
myscript.sh ¦ ➥mail foo@foo.com	Mail the output of the script to foo@foo.com.

<

<   Reads from a file, sending the contents to the standard input of a command.

Example	Description
mail foo@foo.com ➥< report.txt	Mail the file report.txt to foo@foo.com.
myprogram < commands.txt	Send the contents of a file to the standard input of a program.

>

>   Sends the output of a command to a file. If the file does not exist, it is created. If it already exists, an error is returned.

Example	Description
grep "com" domains.txt > commercial.txt	Find all lines that contain "com" in the file called domains.txt and put them in a file called commercial.txt.
myprogram > output.txt	Send the output of a program to a file.

>>

Appends the output of a command or script to a file. If the file does not exist, an error is returned.

Example	Description
echo "The last line." >> somefile.txt	Echo a string and append it to the end of a file.
myprogram &>> myprogram.out	Append all output including stderr to a file.

tee

/usr/bin/tee [*options*] [*files*]

The tee utility acts like a tee in plumbing: It effectively splits standard output into two streams. This command can be useful in some cases, especially those in which the input from a program must be viewed on the screen and sent to a file at the same time. The output can also be appended to more than one file by specifying multiple files on the command line. The output of tee is not buffered. If the file specified exists and the -a option is not given, the file will be overwritten.

Option	Description
-a	Append. The output of tee is appended to the specified file rather than overwriting it.
-I	Interrupts are ignored.

Example	Description
csh ¦ tee -a logfile &	Record a log of a command shell.
myscript.sh ¦ tee ➥-a myscript.out	Send the output of a shell script to the screen and a file.

Logical Operations

case/switch

Choose from among a list of options. Usually a variable is read in using read, and then case is used to act, depending on what the value of read was.

Options can also be complex expressions, such as *option1¦option2* (*option1* or *option2*).

sh Syntax

```
case $VARIABLE in
        option1)              action1;;
        option2)              action2;;
        option3)              action3;;
        optionn)              actionn;;
esac
```

csh Syntax

```
switch ($VARIABLE)
        case option1:
                          action1
                          breaksw
        case option2:
                          action2
                          breaksw
        case optionn:
                          actionn
                          endsw
endsw
```

ksh Syntax

```
case $VARIABLE in
        option1)              action1;;
        option2)              action2;;
        option3)              action3;;
        optionn)              actionn;;
esac
```

csh Example

The following is an example of how to use the switch command in the csh shell. The example would echo the full department name based on a key letter.

```
switch ($DEPT)
        case "S":
                          echo "Sales Department"
                          breaksw
        case "M":
                          echo "Marketing Department"
                          breaksw
        case default:
                          echo "Invalid dept. code"
                          endsw
endsw
```

if-then-else

Test a condition or expression and perform an action based on the results.   if-then-else
The if statement can be simple, or it can use **else** statements to provide
more alternative actions.

sh Syntax

```
if condition; then action; fi
or
if condition; then action; else action2; fi
```

csh Syntax

```
if (condition1) then
action
else if (condition2) then
action2
else
action3
endif
```

ksh Syntax

```
if condition; then action; fi
or
if condition; then action; else action2; fi
```

Example	**Task**
if [$A -gt $B]	Test if the variable A is greater than the variable B.
if [$A -gt $B] [$A -lt $C]	Test if the variable A is greater than the variable B and if the variable A is less than the variable C.

Loops

do-while   sh csh ksh

Loop a series of actions or commands until a specified condition is met.   do-while

sh Syntax

```
while condition ; do actions  ; done
```

csh Syntax
```
while (conditions)
actions
end
```

ksh Syntax
```
while condition ; do actions  ; done
```

Example
```
cat userlist.txt ¦ while read USER
do
    mail $USER < mailmsg.txt
done
```

Read usernames from a text file and send the message stored in
mailmsg.txt to each one.

exit   sh csh ksh

exit   Terminate script and exit with the given exit status.

sh Syntax
```
exit n
```

csh Syntax
```
exit (expression)
```

ksh Syntax
```
exit n
```

n is the exit status (optional). The C Shell can evaluate an expression to
determine the number to return for the exit status.

foreach   sh csh ksh

foreach   Repeat a set of actions once for every occurrence of the *key* in the *list*.

sh Syntax
```
for key in list...  ; do actions ; done
```

csh **Syntax**

```
foreach key (list)
    ...
end

repeat count command
```

ksh **Syntax**

```
for key in list ...; do actions ; done
```

goto   csh

Shell command to force scripts to process steps out of order.   goto

Syntax

```
goto label
```

label is a label somewhere else in the script of the form label:.

3
Process Control

Starting Processes

at

/usr/bin/at [*options*] [*arguments*]
/usr/bin/batch [*options*] [*arguments*]

Queue commands to be run at a specific time in the future. The job will
be run using a different instance of the user shell. Any output sent to
standard out will be mailed to the user. Jobs are spooled to /var/spool/
cron/atjobs.

After a job has been sucessfully queued, a status message similar to the
following will be returned:

commands will be executed using /usr/sbin/tcsh
job 917486999.a at Wed Feb 27 20:29:59 1998

Option	Description
-c	Run command with csh (C shell).
-f *file*	Use *file* as the job rather than standard input.
-k	Run command with ksh (Korn shell).
-l	List all scheduled jobs.
-m	Notify the user by mail when the job has been run.
-q *queue*	Specify a queue to put the job in or to list with -l. The queues are named with single characters—letters a through z.
-r *id*	Remove the job with the job ID specified by *id*.
-s	Run command with sh (Bourne shell).
-t *time*	Run job at *time*.

Arguments

The following arguments can be used in conjunction with any of the
previous options:

Argument	Description
Job Id	Job IDs are reported when jobs are originally scheduled by the at command.

continues >>

Argument	Description
Time	Time values can be specified in 12-hour format (when used with AM or PM following the time) or in 24-hour format. The tokens midnight, noon, and now are also supported.

Example	Description
at now + 1 hour myscript.sh <EOT>	Run a command one hour from now.
at now tomorrow myscript.sh <EOT>	Run a command tomorrow.

▶ **See Also** crontab (56), atrm (55), atq (55)

atrm

/usr/bin/atrm   atrm

Remove jobs that were previously queued by at or batch.

Option	Description
-a	Remove all jobs from the queue.
-f	Force all informational messages to be suppressed.
-I	Interactively ask for confirmation for each job before it is removed.

▶ **See Also** at (54), crontab (56), atq (55)

atq

/usr/bin/atq   atq

List jobs queued using the at or batch command.

Option	Description
-c	List jobs in the order in which they were queued. (List by creation date/time.)
-n	Display the total number of queued jobs.

Example	Description
atq -c	Show all pending jobs, in the order in which they were queued.
atq -n	Check how many jobs are currently queued.

▶ **See Also** at (54), atrm (55), crontab (56)

crontab

crontab   /usr/bin/crontab [*filename*]
             /usr/bin/ [*options*] [*user*]

Utility to manage a user's crontab file. The crontab file is used by cron to run jobs at scheduled times.

Option	Description
-e	Edit the current crontab file. The default editor is ed, but can be changed by setting the EDITOR environment variable to the path and name of the editor to use.
-l	List all entries in the crontab file.
-r	Remove all entries in the crontab file.

Date and Time Formats

[*minute*] [*hour*] [*day of month*] [*month*] [*day of week*]

Date or Time	Valid values
minute	0 to 59
hour	0 to 23
day of month	1 to 31
month	1 to 12
day of week	0 to 6 (Sunday is 0, Monday is 1, and so on.)

An asterisk (*) in place of any of the date/time fields means "all." A list of dates or times can be given by separating the times with commas, such as in the examples that follow:

Example	Description
0 2 * * 1-5 /home/home/ ➥mybackup.sh	Perform a task every weekday at 2:00 AM (such as run a backup).

continues >>

Example	Description
`0 12 1,15 * * /home/` `➥smithj/ mytask`	Run a task on the first and fifteenth of each month at 12 noon.
`0,10,20,30,40,50 * * * * /` `➥home/smithj/checkbot`	Run a task every ten minutes, every hour, every day.
`0 0 7 2 * /home/mulligaj/` `➥bday.sh 2>&1 > /dev/null`	Run a task on February 7th and suppress any mail that might be sent to the user.
`0 17 * * * /home/smithj/` `➥mytask &¦ mail smithj`	Run a task each night at 5:00 PM and mail all output (including standard error) to the user.

▶ **See Also** atq (55), atrm (55), ed (11)

nice

```
/usr/bin/nice [options] command
/usr/xpg4/bin/nice [options] command
```
nice

Run a command with modified scheduling for better CPU usage.
`/usr/bin/nice` uses `/usr/bin/sh` to execute commands.
`/usr/xpg4/bin/nice` uses `/usr/bin/ksh` to execute commands.

Option	Description
-n	Set priority to *n* where *n* is 1...19 (19 is low priority, 1 is high priority). Default is 10.

Examples

`nice -n 1 mycommand`	Run a command with a very high priority.
`nice -n 19 mycommand`	Run a command with a very low priority.

▶ **See Also** nice (57), ps (61)

time

```
/usr/bin/time [options] command
```
time

Time a command in seconds. The following statistics are given: Elapsed time, User CPU time, System CPU time.

Option	Description
-p	Reformat the output of the time command to be one of the following: ■ real *realtime* ■ user *usertime* ■ sys *systime*

Example	Description
time ls	Time the ls command.
time sh -c 'grep key ➥file¦uniq -c¦sort'	Time a more complicated command.

▶ **See Also** time× (58), ps (61)

timex

timex   /usr/bin/timex [*options*] *command*

Time a command. The following statistics are given: Elapsed time, user time, system time, and process accounting data.

Option	Description
-o	If process accounting software is installed, give the number of blocks read/written during execution of the command.
-p	Process accounting. This command only works if process accounting software has been installed.
-f	Must be used with -p. Display exit status flags as well.
-h	Must be used with -p. Display the hog factor calculated as (*total CPU time*) ÷ (*elapsed time*).
-k	Must be used with -p. Give kcore minutes.
-m	Must be used with -p. Display mean core size.
-r	Must be used with -p. Display (*user time*) ÷ (*system-time* + *user-time*).
-t	Must be used with -p. Separate system and user times in the output.
-s	Return the total system time elapsed during the execution of the command.

▶ **See Also** time (57), ps (61)

Process Status

bg

bg [*job-id*]   bg

This is a built-in shell command used to control processes. Therefore, this command will behave slightly differently for each shell.

Shell	Function
sh	Resume a process that previously has been stopped. A job ID can be specified on the command line. If one is not given, the current job is used.
csh	Run the current or specified job(s) in the background. When a suspended job ID is specified, it is the same as running the job followed by an ampersand (&).
ksh	Resume a suspended job and run it in the background.

Example	Description
bg 2	Run the process with a job ID of 2 in the background.
bg	Resume the current process, running it in the background.

▶ **See Also** fg (59), jobs (60)

fg

fg [*job-id*]   fg

This is a shell-specific command, and therefore it behaves slightly differently for each shell. The basic function is to run a process in the foreground.

Shell	Function
sh	Move a suspended or background job to the foreground.
csh	Move the current or specified job to the foreground.
ksh	Move the current or specified job to the foreground.

Example	Description
fg 5	Move the process with a job ID of **5** to the foreground.
fg	Move the current suspended job to the foreground.

▶ **See Also** bg (59), jobs (60)

history

history   Lists the last 16 commands.

jobs

jobs   jobs [*options*] [*job-id*]

Built-in shell job control. Options work slightly differently depending on which shell is used.

Options

Shell	Command	Description
Sh	-l	List the process group IDs and working directories of each job.
	-p	Same as -l but list only group IDs.
	-x *command* [*options*]	Replace each job ID found in command with the process group ID, and then run *command*.
Csh	-l	List the process IDs of each job.
Ksh	-l	List the job ID, current job, process group ID, state, and command that started the job, for each job.
	-n	Notify user of jobs that have exited since the last notification.
	-p	Similar to -l, but only list process IDs for leaders of jobs.

▶ **See Also** at (54), bg (59), stop (65), fg (59)

ps

/usr/bin/ps [*options*]   ps

Display information about processes currently running.

Option	Description
-a	List all processes that are not group leaders.
-A	List all processes.
-c	Format output as described in priocntl.
-d	List all processes except session leaders.
-e	List all processes that are currently active.
-f	Format output as a full listing.
-g *grouplist*	List processes for listed group leaders.
-G *gidlist*	List processes that have a realgroup ID listed in *gidlist*.
-j	List processes, including session ID and group ID.
-l	Format output as a long listing.
-o *format*	Format output as specified by *format*.
-p *proclist*	List processes of those with process ID numbers specified in *proclist*.
-s *sidlist*	List processes for all session leaders listed in *sidlist*.
-t *term*	List all processes connected to the terminal specified by *term*.
-u *uidlist*	List all processes with the same effective UID as those given in *uidlist*.
-U *uidlist*	List all processes with the same real UID as those listed in *uidlist*.

Output Headings

Heading	Description
F	Flags
S	State
	■ O: Running on CPU
	■ S: Sleeping

continues >>

>>continued

Heading	Description
	▪ R: Runnable
	▪ Z: Zombie
	▪ T: Stopped
UID	Effective user ID
PID	Process ID
PPID	Parent's process ID
C	CPU usage for scheduling
CLS	Scheduling class
PRI	Priority
NI	nice value
ADDR	Memory address
SZ	Size of swappable image (given in pages)
WCHAN	The address of the process that the listed process is waiting for
STIME	Start time
TTY	Controlling terminal
TIME	Total active time for the process
CMD	Full command name
PGID	Process group leader PID
SID	Session leader PID

▶ **See Also** at (54), atq (55), kill (64)

ps (UCB version)

ps (UCB version)

/usr/ucb/ps [*options*]

Show process information.

Option	Description
-a	List all processes, excluding process group leaders.
-c	List processes with more reliable command name information.

continues >>

Option	Description
-g	List all processes including process group leaders.
-l	Format as a long listing: F, PPID, CP, PRI, NI, SZ, RSS, and WCHAN.
-n	Replace USER field with UID (numerical format).
-r	List on running processes.
-s	Display total CPU time for processes, including child times.
-t *term*	List processes controlled by the terminal specified by *term*.
-u	Format as user listing: USER, SZ, RSS, or START.
-U	Update ps database.
-v	Display virtual memory.
-w	Wide output format, using 132 characters (rather than 80).
-x	List processes that have no controlling terminal.
-ww	No limits on output width.

Output Headings

Heading	Description
CP	CPU usage factor (short–term)
F	Flags ■ 00: Terminated ■ 01: System process ■ 02: Tracing parent ■ 04: Parent is waiting ■ 08: Process in main memory ■ 10: Process locked in main memory
NI	Niceness
PPID	Parent PID
PRI	Priority
RSS	Resident memory size in KB
SIZE/SZ	Size in KB (*stack* + *data*)

continues >>

>>continued

Heading	Description
START	Start time
UID	UID of process owner
USER	Username of process owner
WCHAN	Address of a process for which a sleeping process is waiting

▶ **See Also** ps (61), nice (57), renice (64)

renice

renice   /usr/bin/renice [*options*] *ID*

Change the priority of a process that is already running.

Option	Description
-g	Treat all operands as unsigned decimal integer process GIDs.
-n *n*	Increment the priority of the process by *n*.
-p	Treat all operands as unsigned decimal integer PIDs.
-u	Treat all operands as users.

Example	Description
renice -n 1 345	Increase the priority of a running process (with PID of 345).
renice -n -1 345	Decrease the priority of a running process.
renice -n 19 345	Maximize the priority of a running process.

▶ **See Also** nice (57), ps (61), kill (64)

Stopping Processes

kill

kill   /usr/bin/kill -s *signal pid-list*
/usr/bin/kill -l [*stat*]
/usr/bin/kill [-*signal*] *pid-list*

Terminate (kill) processes or send special signals to processes. Use ps to obtain process ID numbers.

Option	Description
-l	List all signals, if no other arguments are given. If an exit status is specified by *stat*, the terminating signal of the process will be displayed.
-s *signal*	Specify the signal to send to the process.

Signals

The following is a list of signals for use with kill (generated from kill -l). For a full description of signals, see Appendix C, "Signals."

ABRT	ALRM	BUS	CLD	CONT	EMT	FPE
FREEZE	HUP	ILL	INT	KILL	LWP	PIPE
POLL	PROF	PWR	QUIT	RTMAX	RTMAX-1	
RTMAX-2	RTMAX-3	RTMIN	RTMIN+1	RTMIN+2	RTMIN+3	
SEGV	STOP	SYS	TERM	THAW	TRAP	
TSTP	TTIN	TTOU	URG	USR1	USR2	
VTALRM	WAITING	WINCH	XCPU	XFSZ		

Examples

`kill -9 102`	Kill a process and all of its children.
`kill -HUP 203`	Restart a process.

`kill -HUP 'ps`
`➥-ax ¦ grep inetd ¦`
`➥grep -v grep ¦`
`➥awk '{print $1}''`
	Restart inetd.

`ps -aux ¦ grep inetd`
`➥¦ grep -v grep ¦ awk`
`➥'{print $1}' ¦xargs`
`➥kill -9`
	Kill all processes belonging to the user smithj.

▶ **See Also** jobs (60), ps (61)

stop

stop [*job-id*]   stop

Stop the job identified by *job-id*. If no ID is given, the background job is stopped.

▶ **See Also** at (54), fg (59), bg (59)

4

Network Clients and Utilities

Informational Utilities

finger

finger

```
/usr/bin/finger [options] [user]
/usr/bin/finger [options] [user@host]
/usr/bin/finger [options] [user@host@host@host.... etc.]
```

Retrieve information about users from the current host or remote servers. The remote server must be running a finger daemon (in.fingerd).

Option	Description
-b	Do not show home directories and shells in the information given.
-f	Do not print headers.
-h	Do not show .project files.
-I	Idle format. Output includes username, terminal, login time, and idle time.
-l	Long format. Output includes all information.
-m	Match user with username and not the full name of the user.
-p	Do not show .plan files.
-q	Quick format. Output includes username, terminal, and login time.
-s	Short format.
-w	Short format without printing full name.

File	Description
.project	Text file that optionally can be kept in the user's home directory. If present, it is printed in the Project field of the finger output.
.plan	Text file that optionally can be kept in the user's home directory. If present, it is printed at the end of the finger information for the user.

Finger Forwarding

Finger forwarding is when a finger request is sent to a remote host and then "forwarded" to another host, where it is processed and the resulting information is sent back to the original sender of the request. Consider the following example:

```
finger smithj@host1.com@host2.com@host3.com
```

The finger request will go from the local host to host3.com.

host3.com will forward the request to host2.com, host2.com will forward the request to host1.com, and host1.com will send the finger information (if available) back to the local host.

In each case, the request will be logged on the remote system as coming from the forwarding host. host1.com will log the request as being from the local host. It is for this reason that some system administrators disable finger forwarding on their servers. This is a recommended practice that can potentially make your entire network more secure.

Finger forwarding is not supported on all servers. The specifications for finger forwarding are defined in RFC 1288.

Example	Description
finger	To retrieve finger information for all users on the local host.
finger smithj	To retrieve finger information for a single user on the local system.
finger @*remotehost*.com	To retrieve finger information for all users on a remote host.
finger smithj @*remotehost*.com	To retrieve finger information for a single user on a remote host.

▶ **See Also** whois (77)

netstat

netstat [*options*] [*interval*]

netstat

Show current network information for the local host. This command can be used to show all network connections to the local system, routing information, and network interface information.

Option	Description
interval	An interval can be specified, causing netstat to report the network status every *interval* seconds. This interval is optional. If omitted, netstat will run once.
-a	All socket and routing table states and entries are shown. If this option is omitted, daemon processes will not be shown and only limited routing table information will be given.
-f *fam*	Only show reports for those that are of the specified family. The family can be either of the following: ■ inet: AF_INET address family ■ unix: AF_UNIX address family
-g	Multicast group memberships for all interfaces are displayed.
-I	Display TCP/IP interface state.
-I *interface*	The current state of the network interface specified by *interface* is shown.
-m	Display statistics for STREAMS.
-M	Multicast routing tables are shown. Can be used with the -s option to give summary statistics using the multicast routing tables.
-n	Do not resolve addresses. This option will cause any hosts to be reported by IP address rather than by hostname. Using this usually greatly increases the speed of the netstat command.
-p	Display address resolution tables (ARP tables).
-p *protocol*	Only show network statistics for sockets using the protocol specified by *protocol*. This can be tcp or udp.
-r	Display routing tables.
-s	Give statistics sorted by protocol, such as tcp or udp. If used with -M, multicast routing statistics are used instead.
-v	Verbose. Reports are given in more detail.

TCP Socket States

State	Description
CLOSED	Closed. The socket has been closed and is not in use.
CLOSE_WAIT	Wait for close. The remote side has closed the connection and the local host is waiting for the socket to close.

continues >>

State	Description
CLOSING	Closing. Socket has been closed and the remote connection has been shut down. The socket is waiting for acknowledgment.
ESTABLISHED	Connection established. A TCP/IP connection is established and working.
FIN_WAIT_1	Finish wait 1. The socket has been successfully closed and is waiting to shut down the connection.
FIN_WAIT_2	Finish wait 2. Socket has been closed and is waiting for remote side to shut down connection.
LAST_ACK	Last acknowledgement. The remote side of the connection has been shut down and closed. Waiting for acknowledgement.
LISTEN	Listening. The socket is currently listening. Programs such as servers and daemons will usually spawn processes that open sockets to listen.
SYN_SENT	Synchronization sent. The socket is attempting to establish a connection with a remote host.
SYN_RECEIVED	Synchronization received. A response has been received after sending a synchronization request. The connection is being made.
TIME_WAIT	Wait after close. Socket has been closed, waiting for remote shutdown retransmission.

Example	Description
netstat	Check what remote hosts are connected to the local system.
netstat -n	Check what remote hosts are connected to the local system, but leave addresses as IP numbers (much faster).

▶ **See Also** rpcinfo (73)

nslookup

/usr/sbin/nslookup [*options*] [*host*] [*DNS server*]   nslookup

Utility to query an Internet domain name server to resolve an IP address to a name or a name to an IP address. By default, nslookup uses the server in /etc/resolv.conf as the DNS server. It can be used in two general ways:

■ Hostname specified on the command line.

■ Run without hostname specified to use interactive mode.

Command–Line Options

Option	Description
-option	Set or change lookup state information. For example: -retry=5 See the later section "State Keywords" for a list.
DNSserver	Specify a DNS server. If no DNS server is given, the one listed in /etc/resolv.conf is used.
host	Host can be either a domain name or an IP address. If a host is specified on the command line, the results are returned and interactive mode is not used.

Interactive Mode Commands

Command	Description
CTRL+D	Exit.
finger[name]	Finger the last host that was successfully looked up.
help	Show a command summary. Using ? is the same as using help.
host [server]	Look up host using server as the DNS server. If server is not given, the DNS server listed in /etc/resolv.conf is used.
ls [-ah]	List all domain name service information for the domain: ■ -a: Show all aliases as well. ■ -h: Show host information including CPU and OS information.
root	Change the default server to ns.nic.ddn.mil.
set	Set a keyword value. Keyword definitions must be of one of the following forms: ■ set keyword ■ set keyword = value See the subsequent "State Keywords" section for a list of all keywords that can be set.
server domain	Change the default server to the domain specified by domain.
view file	Use more to view the given file.

State Keywords

Keyword	Description
all	Show all set keywords and their values.
debug or nodebug	Turn debugging on or off. The default is nodebug.
defname or nodefname	If defname is set, the default domain name is appended to every hostname that is looked up. The default is nodefname.
domain = file	Change the default domain to file. If no file is given, the domain given in /etc/resolv.conf is used.
querytype = type	Set query type (specified in RFC 833): ■ A: Host Internet address (default) ■ CNAME: Canonical name ■ HINFO: Host CPU and OS type ■ MD: Mail destination ■ MX: Mail exchanger ■ MB: Mailbox domain name ■ MG: Mail group member ■ MINFO: Mailbox or mail list information
recurse or norecurse	If recurse is set and the current server does not have the information, it will check other servers. The default is recurse.
retry=n	Retry the request n times if the initial request fails.
root=host	Change the root server (default is ns.nic.ddn.mil) to host.
timeout= seconds	Set the timeout for a query to the number of seconds specified by seconds.
vc or novc	Force the use of a virtual circuit. The default is novc.

▶ **See Also** whois (77)

rpcinfo

/usr/bin/rcpinfo [*options*] [*host*] [*prog*] [*version*]   rpcinfo

Use RPC calls to report RPC information. RPC information for both local and remote hosts can be reported. In general, rpcinfo can be used in three ways:

- List all registered RPC services on a host.
- List all `rpcbind` version 2 registered RPC services on a host.
- Make a call (procedure 0) to a specific program on a host.

Option	Description
-a *addr*	Use the address specified by *addr* as the universal address for the service. Used to `ping` a remote service.
-b	Broadcast procedure 0 of the service listed and report all responses from the network that are received.
-d	Delete a service registration for the specified program and version number.
-l	List entries matching the specified program and version number on a host.
-m	Show summary statistics for `rcpbind` on a remote host. Statistics for `rcpbind` versions 2, 3, and 4 are shown.
-p	Probe. The host is probed using version 2 of the `rpcbind` protocol. If a host is specified, that host is probed. If no host is specified, the local host is probed.
-s	Short list. Give a short list of all RPC programs registered on the specified remote host, or on the local host if no remote host is specified.
-T *transport*	Require the RPC service to be on the transport specified by *transport*. If this option is omitted, the transport in the environment variable NETPATH is used. If NETPATH is not set, the `netconfig` database is used to determine the transport.

Example	Description
`rpcinfo`	Check what RPC services are registered on the local host.
`rpcinfo` *remotehost*	Check what RPC services are registered on a remote host.
`rpcinfo -p` *remotehost*	Check what RPC services are registered on a remote host, showing only version 2 programs.

ping

Uses the Internet Control Message Protocol to check whether a remote host is alive on the network.

Local host →ECHO_REQUEST→ Remote host

Local host ←ECHO_RESPONSE← Remote host

Command	Description
-I *interface*	Use the interface specified by *interface* for outgoing packets.
-I *n*	Interval. Wait *n* seconds between pings.
-l	Loose source route. The packet will find a route to the destination host. Using this option, the reply packet will discover a route back to the originating host (not necessarily the same as the original route). This can be used to diagnose possible routing problems between two hosts on a network.
-L	No loopback of multicast packets. Do not copy multicast packets to members of the host group of the interface.
-n	Numerical addresses. Show IP numbers for hosts rather than DNS names.
-r	Skip routing tables. Packet is sent directly to host. This only works if the remote host is on the same network segment.
-R	Route recording. The route of the packet is stored in the IP header.
-t *livetime*	Time to live for packets is set to *livetime*. The default is one hop.
-v	Verbose output. List all ICMP packets received.

Example

Test connectivity as seen by NFS packets. Show degradation in passing through alternative packet-sized routing equipment.

```
ping -sv hostname 8192
```

▶ **See Also** whois (77)

rup

/usr/sbin/rup [*options*] [*host*]

Similar to the uptime command, but displays information for remote hosts. If no host is specified, the request is broadcast to all machines. Remote systems must be running the rstatd daemon to respond. Note that ruptime uses the in.rwhod daemon, whereas rup uses the rstatd daemon.

Option	Description
-h	Sort output by host name.
-l	Sort output by load average.
-t	Sort output by uptime.

▶ **See Also** ruptime (76)

ruptime

/usr/bin/ruptime [*options*]

Check information for a remote host. Information given is similar to that of uptime. Each machine on the local network is queried and a response must be received within five minutes. The remote server must be running the remote who daemon (in.rwhod). Note that ruptime uses the in.rwhod daemon, whereas rup uses the rstatd daemon.

Option	Description
-a	Include all users in the output. If omitted, any user idle for more than an hour will be excluded.
-l	Output sorted by load average.
-r	Output given in reverse order.
-t	Output sorted by uptime.
-u	Output sorted by number of users.

▶ **See Also** rwho (82), rusers (77)

rusers

/usr/bin/rusers [*options*] [*host*]   rusers

A remote version of who to find out who is logged in to a remote host.
More than one host can be specified on the command line. If no hosts are
specified, rusers sends out a broadcast for rusersd protocol, version 3.
This is followed by a broadcast of version 2. Hosts must be running the
ruserd daemon in order to respond.

Option	Description
-a	Report machines even with no users logged in.
-h	Alphabetically list hosts.
-i	Reports are sorted by idle time.
-l	Long report format, giving more detail.
-u	Reports are sorted by the number of users logged in.

▶ **See Also** rwall (88), rwho (82)

whois

/usr/bin/whois [*options*] [*string*]   whois

Check the InterNIC database for a domain record or records. If an exact
match is found for the string, the domain record for the domain is printed.
If the string matches multiple domains, summaries of the domains are
shown. Other NICs can be checked by specifying the host using the -h
option.

Example	Description
whois *somedomain.com*	Check if a domain is registered and/or find out contact and billing information for the domain.
whois [*string*]	Find all domains containing a certain string.

Option	Description
-h	Specify which host to use for lookups to find information at other NICs (optional).

▶ **See Also** finger (68)

File Transfers

ftp

ftp   /usr/bin/ftp [*options*] [*host*]

File Transfer Protocol (FTP) client to upload and download files over the network. If no host is specified on the command line, an ftp> command prompt is given. The remote server must be running an FTP daemon (in.ftpd).

Option	Description
-d	Debugging mode.
-g	Do not use filename globbing.
-I	Do not ask for confirmation for each file of a multiple file transfer (non-interactive mode).
-n	Disable auto-login.
-v	Verbose. Show all diagnostics and give a summary of data transfer statistics.

Command	Description
? *command*	Same as help.
! *command*	Run *command* using the shell. If no command is given, the shell is used as the command interpreter until **exit** is typed.
$ *macro*	Run the macro specified by *macro*. See macdef, later in this table.
account *password*	Provide an extra password to the remote system if necessary. If no password is given, the user is prompted for one.
append *file1* *file2*	Append the local file *file1* to the remote file, *file2*.
ascii	Set the transfer mode to ASCII (rather than binary).
bell	Toggle beeping after each file transfer.
binary	Set the transfer mode to binary (rather than ASCII).
bye	Close session and exit.

continues >>

Command	Description
case	Toggle case mapping. Default is off. ■ on: All uppercase characters on the remote system are changed to lowercase. ■ off: No changes are made to uppercase or lowercase characters.
cd *dir*	Change directories on the remote host to *dir*.
cdup	Change the current directory on the remote host to the parent directory.
close	Close FTP session.
cr	Toggle carriage-return (CR) stripping during ASCII mode.
delete *file*	Delete file on the remote host.
debug	Toggle debugging mode. Default is off.
dir	Give a directory listing of the current remote host working directory. Output is similar to that of ls.
disconnect	Same as close.
get *file* *filename*	Download the file specified by *file* from the remote host to the local host. If *filename* is given, that name is used on the local host. If not, the remote name is used.
glob	Toggle globbing for use with mdelete, mget, and mput. Globbing is filename expansion, the same as done by sh.
hash	Toggle hash marks (#). If on, hash marks will usually be printed for every 8,192 bytes transferred. Some systems may use a different hash mark size, in which case it will be specified. Another common hash mark size is 2,048 bytes.
help *command*	Give help on *command*. If no command is specified, a list of commands is displayed.
lcd *dir*	Change local directory to *dir*.
ls	Similar to dir, but gives a briefer directory listing. If the -a option is given, all files are listed, including those that begin with a dot (.).
macdef *macro*	Define a macro by the name of *macro*. Input following macdef will be stored as the macro until a newline is given.

continues >>

Command	Description
mdelete *files*	Multiple delete. Delete the file or files given by *files*.
mdir *files*	Multiple directory listing. List the files or directories specified.
mget *files*	Multiple get. Download all the files specified.
mkdir *dir*	Make directory. Create a directory on the remote system called *dir*.
mls *files*	Multiple ls. Same as ls, but more than one file or directory can be given.
mput *files*	Multiple put. Upload all of the files specified.
open *host port*	Open a connection with host on port. If no port is given, 21/tcp is used.
prompt	Toggle interactive prompting. If this is off, no prompt will be given between file transfers when using mput or mget.
proxy *command*	Run command on a secondary server. This can be used to transfer files between two remote servers.
put *file filename*	Upload file to the remote host. If filename is given, it is renamed to filename on the remote host. If no filename is given, the original filename is used on the remote server.
pwd	Print the current working directory.
quit	Same as bye.
quote *args*	Send the specified file directly to the remote FTP server.
recv *file*	Same as get.
remotehelp	Same as help, but the remote server rather than the local server is used to obtain help.
rename *old new*	Rename the file specified by *old* from *old* to *new*.
reset	Clear the reply queue.
rmdir *dir*	Remove the directory on the remote server specified by *dir*.
runique	Toggle unique filenames. If it is on, and a duplicate filename is found, the new file will have a *.n* appended to it, where *n* is an integer that increments up starting at 1.

continues >>

Command	Description
send *file*	Same as put.
status	Display current status.
sunique	Remote unique file naming. Refer to runique, earlier in this table.
type *type*	Set transfer type to *type*. Either binary (image) or ASCII (text).
user *username*	Give username to the remote system when logging in.
verbose	Toggle verbose mode. If verbose mode is on, all FTP server responses are shown.

FTP Autologin

A .netrc file can be placed in a user home directory to allow ftp file transfers to be automated to some extent. The file contains information about the connection including the hostname, login name, password, and other optional information.

The general format is as follows:

```
machine hostname login loginname password password
```

Consider the following example:

```
machine ftp.remotehost.com login anonymous password
➥user@localhost.com
```

It is very important that .netrc file permissions are set so that other users cannot access the file because it contains account names and passwords. Use the chmod command to set the .netrc file to mode 600.

▶ See Also rcp (81)

rcp

/usr/bin/rcp [*options*] [*files*]   rcp

Copy files across a network. In order to use rcp, remote commands must be allowed by using rsh. This requires the use of a .rhosts file or /etc/hosts.equiv. See rsh for details.

Option	Description
-p	Attempt to preserve all the file properties of the original, giving the copy the same time, mode, and ACL if possible.
-r	Recursively copy the directory specified by the *files* argument.

Arguments

The arguments of rcp are specified as remote files or local files.

For local files:

    path

For remote files:

    host:path
    user@host:path

Using **rcp** with Symbolic Links

rcp cannot properly copy directories containing symbolic links . A possible alternative is to use cpio to pipe the directory to rcp.

Example	Description
rcp *remotehost:* *testfile testfile*	Copy a file from a remote machine to the local host.
rcp *remote1:report*.txt *remote2:newreport*.txt	Copy a file between two remote machines (third-party copy).

▶ **See Also** rsh (91), ftp (78)

rwho

rwho   /usr/bin/rwho [*options*]

List who is logged on to machines on the local network. Output is similar to that of who. The remote server must be running the in.rwhod daemon.

▶ **See Also** rusers (77), finger (68)

Communications

mail

/usr/bin/mail [*options*] [*recipient*]   mail

Utility to read or send (using sendmail) electronic mail to users on the
local system and over the Internet. If mail is run with no recipient given, it
can be used to read and process mail. A question mark (?) will be given as a
command prompt. If mail exits while a message is being composed, it will
be saved to dead.letter in the current directory. Incoming mail is saved in
/var/mail/*username* or at a location specified in the MAIL variable, where
username is the current login name of the user running mail.

Option	Description
-e	Mail is not printed. However, mail returns an error code:
	■ 1 if there is no mail.
	■ 0 if there is mail.
-f *file*	Use the file specified by *file* as the mailfile rather than the default.
-h	Show headers instead of latest message when starting.
-m *type*	Add a header to the message of the form:
	Messsage-Type: *type*
-p	Print all messages without checking dispositions.
-P	Print all headers when displaying messages.
-q	Quit and exit when an interrupt is received.
-r	Print messages in "first-in, first-out" order.
-t	Add a header to the message (for each recipient) of the form:
	To: *recipient*
-w	Do not wait for remote transfer program to exit before sending.
-x *level*	Set debugging level to *level* (creates a tracefile in /tmp).

Command	Description
?	Help. Displays all commands with their usages.
#	Print the current message number.
-	Previous message.
+ or *newline*	Next message.
!*command*	Use the shell to run *command*.
a	Display a message that arrived since mail was started.
d	d or dp: Delete the current message and display the next one.
	d *n*: Delete message number *n*.
	dq: Delete the current message and then quit.
h	h: Show headers for current message.
	h *n*: Show headers for message number *n*.
	h a: Show headers for all messages.
	h d: Show headers for messages marked for deletion.
m *recipient*	Send the current message to *recipient*, and delete it.
number	Go to message number *n*.
p	Reprint the current message, ignoring non-printable characters.
P	Reprint current message showing all headers.
q or **CTRL+D**	Quit. Any messages that were marked for deletion are not deleted.
r *recipients*	Reply to sender. If *recipients* are specified, they are carbon-copied on the mail.
s *mailfile*	Save messages in the file specified by *mailfile*. Default file is mbox.
u *n*	Undelete message number *n*. If no number is given, the last message read is undeleted.
w *file*	Write the current message to *file*, suppressing any headers. If no file is given, mbox is used.
x	Save all messages and exit.
y *file*	Same as w.

▶ **See Also** write (90)

mail (UCB version)

/usr/ucb/mail [*options*] *users*

/usr/ucb/mail

Use the UCB version of the mail utility to read or send (using **sendmail**) electronic mail to users on the local system and over the Internet. If mail is run with no recipient given, it can be used to read and process mail. A **?** will be given as a command prompt. If mail exits while a message is being composed, it will be saved to **dead.letter** in the current directory. Incoming mail is saved in **/var/mail/*username*** or at a location specified in the **MAIL** variable in which *username* is the current login name of the user running mail.

Option	Description
-B	No buffer. Neither standard input nor standard output.
-b *bcc*	Blind carbon copy. Blind carbon copy the users in the list *bcc*. More than one recipient may be listed, but they must be enclosed in quotes.
-c *cc*	Carbon copy. Carbon copy the users in the list *cc*. More than one recipient may be listed, but they must be enclosed in quotes.
-d	Debug. Extra debugging information is given.
-e	Test for mail. No output is given. A return value is given indicating the presence of mail: ■ **0**: Mail ■ **1**: No mail
-F	The message is recorded in a file with the same name as the recipient.
-f *msgfile*	Read messages out of the file specified by *msgfile* rather than the default mailbox file.
-H	Header summary. Only message headers are shown.
-h *num*	Set the maximum number of "network hops" to *num*. Setting this option will prevent endless mail loops.
-I	Include newsgroup and article-id headers.
-N	No initial header summary.

continues >>

>>continued

Option	Description
-n	The system default rc files (mailx.rc and Mail.rc) are not read upon startup.
-r *addr*	Set the message return address to *addr*.
-s *subject*	Set the message subject to *subject*. To be safe, the subject should be enclosed in quotes.
-T *file*	The message-id and article-id headers are saved to the file specified by *file*.
-t	Obtain To:, cc:, and bcc: fields from the message text rather than from the command line recipient list.
-u *user*	Use the mailbox of *user*, rather than the current user mailbox.
-V	Display mail version number and exit.

Command	Description
!*cmd*	Execute the given shell command. If no command is given, a command shell is spawned—type **exit** to return to mail.
=	Display the current message number.
?	Display command summary.
alias *alias recip*	Make an alias for the specified mail recipient. Usually aliases are defined in the .mailrc file.
cd *dir*	Change directory to *dir*.
copy *file*	Same as the save command. However, the message is not marked as saved.
delete *msgs*	Delete the listed messages. If no messages are listed, the current message is deleted.
discard *headers*	Discard specified *headers* when displaying messages.
ignore *headers*	Do not print the specified *headers* when displaying messages.
dp *msgs*	Delete-print. Delete the specified messages and then print the next message.
edit *msgs*	Edit the messages using the editor specified in the EDITOR environment variable.

continues >>

Command	Description
exit	Exit mail.
field *header*	Display the contents of the header specified by *header*.
file *file*	Switch mailbox files to *file*. If no file is specified, the current filename is displayed.
followup *msg*	Reply to the author of the specified message.
from *msgs*	Print the header summary of *msgs*. If no messages are specified, print the header summary for the current message.
hold *msgs*	Hold the listed messages in the current mailbox.
inc	Incorporate new messages that arrive in the current mail list.
load *file*	Load the specified file as a mail message. The file must be in a standard single message format, with headers.
mail *recip*	Send a message to the specified recipient.
Mail *recip*	Send a message to the specified recipient and save a copy.
more *msgs*	Display the listed messages, pausing after each page.
Unread *msgs*	Mark the listed messages as unread.
next	Jump to the next message in the message list.
pipe *msgs* *command*	Pipe the listed messages through the specified command.
print *msgs*	Print the specified messages.
put *msgs* *file*	Write the specified messages to the specified file.
quit	Quit. Messages that were saved in a file are deleted; all others are saved.
reply *msgs*	Reply to each message specified. The subject line is taken from the first message in the list of messages.
replyall *msg*	Reply to the message, sending a copy to every recipient of the original message.
Save	Save the specified message, all addressing information is stripped.
save	Save the specified message to the mailbox file (usually mbox).
source *file*	Execute the commands in the specified file.

continues >>

>>continued

Command	Description
shell	Spawn a shell to run commands. Type exit to return to mail.
top *msgs*	Display only the first few lines (top) of the listed messages.
unalias *aliases*	Remove an alias definition. Refer to alias, earlier in this table.
undelete *msgs*	Undelete the listed messages.
unignore	No longer ignore the specified headers. Refer to ignore, earlier in this table.
version	Display the current version of mail.
visual	Edit the message in visual mode. The editor given in the VISUAL environment variable is used. If this variable is not set, vi is used.

rwall

rwall   /usr/sbin/rwall [*options*] [*host*]

Broadcast a message to all users on a network. The message, when received, will be preceded by the following header:

Broadcast Message...

The remote server must be running the walld daemon.

Option	Description
-n *netgroup*	Broadcast the message to the network specified by *netgroup*, rather than to a specific host.
-h *host*	Specify a single host to broadcast the message to. This option can be used in conjunction with the -n option.

▶ **See Also** rwho (82), rusers (77)

talk

talk   /usr/bin/talk *user* [*terminal*]

Talk to other users using the UNIX talk protocol. It can be used to chat with another user on the same system or with other users across the Internet. The remote system must be running a talk daemon (in.talkd) listening on port 517/udp.

When connecting to a remote system, the other user will be prompted to talk with a message similar to the following:

```
Message from Talk_Daemon@remotehost at 8:55 ...
talk: connection requested by
mulligan@localhost.
talk: respond with: talk mulligan@localhost
```

After the other user responds, chatting can begin. The text is sent character by character.

Argument	Description
user	The login name of the user to talk to. It can either be a username (for the local system), or an Internet address of the form user@remotehost for Internet chatting.
terminal	Optional. If a user is logged in more than once, this specifies which terminal to talk to.

Command	Description
CTRL+L	Refresh the screen.
CTRL+D or **CTRL+C**	End the talk session and quit.

▶ **See Also** write (90), mail (83)

wall

/usr/sbin/wall [*options*] [*file*]   wall

Broadcast a message to all users on the local system, in a manner similar to write. All users will see a message similar to the following:

```
Broadcast Message from mulligan (pts/8) on ns1 Wed Apr 12
➥20:24:52...
```

If a file is specified, the contents of the file will be written as the message. If no file is specified, a message can be typed, line by line, until a **CTRL+D** is sent.

The other user on the system must have writeable terminals in order for the wall command to work. Therefore, only the root user can usually use this command to broadcast messages to all the users on a system.

To make `wall` usable by all users, make it `setuid root` using the following command as root:

```
chmod 4755 /usr/sbin/wall
```

This should only be done on a system on which all of the users are trusted not to abuse the `wall` utility.

Option	Description
-a	Broadcast message to all terminals—console and pseudo-terminals.
-g *group*	Broadcast only to the group specified by *group*.

▶ **See Also** `write` (90), `rwall` (88)

write

write | `/usr/bin/write [terminal]`

Send a message to another user on the local system. Unlike `talk`, the text is sent line by line.

When used, `write` will send a message similar to the following to the other user:

```
Message from mulligan on host (pts/6) [ Tue Mar  4 09:11:22 ]
➥...
```

To stop sending messages, press **CTRL+D** or **CTRL+C**.

Argument	Description
terminal	Optional. If the other user is logged in more than once, this specifies which terminal to send the message to.

▶ **See Also** `talk` (88), `mail` (83)

Remote Shells and Login

rlogin

rlogin | `/usr/bin/rlogin [options] [host]`

Description

Log in to a remote system using the remote login procedures rather than telnet. The user and/or host must be defined in a .rhosts or hosts.equiv file on the remote system. The remote server must be running the in.rlogind daemon.

Option	Description
-L	Litout mode.
-8	Use 8-bit data instead of 7-bit.
-e char	Set escape character to char.
-l username	Use username as the username for remote login rather than the current one.

▶ **See Also** telnet (92), rcp (81)

rsh

/usr/bin/rsh [options] [hostname] [command]   rsh

The remote shell executes commands on a remote system across the network. Alternatively, if no command is given, rsh behaves like rlogin and will log the user in to the remote system. This command uses the .rhosts or /etc/hosts.equiv file on the remote system to check if remote execution/login is allowed.

Option	Description
-l username	Use the username specified by username for logging in rather than the current username.
-n	Suppress standard output from rsh. Output is sent to /dev/null.

.rhosts and hosts.equiv

Two files are used to check authentication for the rlogin, rsh, and rcp programs: .rhosts and hosts.equiv. The .rhosts file is placed in a user home directory and lists the hosts and users that are allowed to log into the local account. The general form of the .rhosts file is as follows:

    hostname username

continues >>

>>continued

If the username is omitted, then all users from the specified host are allowed. Optionally, a *netgroup* can be used in place of the username by specifying it as +@*netgroup*. The symbol + is used to represent "all." For example, the following allows remote logins from the user smithj from any host:

```
+ smithj
```

However, this leaves the account open to security exploits and should not be used.

The /etc/hosts.equiv file can be thought of as an .rhosts file for the entire system. If a remote user is allowed to log in based on the host.equiv file, she will be allowed to log in as any local user.

Note that the .rhosts and /etc/hosts.equiv files are two of the most common sources of security breaches. To be safe, follow these recommendations:

- Always use the *hostname username* form; never specify only a user or a host.

- Never use a + in an entry.

- Only list hosts that are completely trusted and very secure.

- Check .rhost and host.equiv files on a regular basis for signs that they have been altered or tampered with in any way.

Example

Display a text file that is located on a remote system:

```
rsh remotehost cat file.txt
```

▶ **See Also** rlogin (90)

telnet

telnet   /usr/bin/telnet [*options*] [*host*] [*port*]

Interface to the telnet protocol to log in to a remote system. telnet can also be used to connect to an arbitrary port/service on a remote host.

Option	Description
-8	Use 8-bit data path.
-E	Suppress all escape characters.

continues >>

Option	Description
-L	Use 8-bit data path on output.
-c	Do not read .telnetrc file.
-d	Toggle debugging mode on.
-e *char*	Set escape character to *char*.
-l *user*	Send the current username as the value of *user*.
-n *file*	Open *file* as a tracefile for the session.
-r	Force telnet to behave more like rlogin. Escape characters: ~, .\r, and **CTRL+Z** can be used (see rlogin).

Command	Description
CTRL-]	Drop back to a prompt. This is very useful when a connection is hung and needs to be terminated. Simply press **CTRL+]** and then type **quit**.
? *command*	Help. Get help on *command*. If *command* is not specified, then a list of commands will be given.
close	Close the current session and exit.
display *arg*	Show values of parameters set by toggle.
environ *args*	Set variables that can be sent to the remote host through environment variables. Arguments include the following: ■ define *variable value* ■ undefine *variable* ■ export ■ unexport *variable* ■ list ■ ?
logout	Same as close, if logout is supported on the remote side.
open *host port*	Open connection to host on port. If no port is given, 23/tcp is used. Optionally, -l user can be added to specify a username other than the current one.
quit	Same as close.

continues >>

>>continued

Command	Description
send *args*	Send *args* (including special characters) to the remote host. Arguments include the following: escape, synch, brk, ip, abort, ao, ayt, ec, el, eof, eor, ga, getstatus, nop, susp.
set or unset *arg value*	Set or unset any of the following arguments: ■ echo: Toggle local echoing. ■ escape: Set escape character to *value*. ■ interrupt: Set interrupt character to *value*. ■ quit: Set quit character. ■ flushoutput: Set flushoutput character. ■ erase: Set erase character. ■ eof: Set eof character. ■ ayt: Set the Are You There character. ■ lnext: Set lnext character in the old line-by-line mode. ■ reprint: Set the reprint character. ■ rlogin: rlogin escape character ■ start: Set start character. ■ stop: Set stop character. ■ susp: Set the suspend character. ■ tracefile: Set the trace file. ■ worderase: Set the worderase character.
status	Display status of telnet.
toggle *args*	Toggles on/off the following parameters: autoflush, autosynch, binary, inbinary, outbinary, crlf, crmod, debug, localchars, netdata, options, prettydump, skiprc, termdata Toggling ? will show all available parameters.
z	Suspend telnet. Job control must be supported.

▶ **See Also** rlogin (90)

II

Administration and Maintenance Task Reference

5

System Configuration and Tuning

System Identification

Changing the System Hostname

Changing
the System
Hostname
It is possible to change the system hostname by using the sys-unconfig utility (See "Reconfiguring the System," p. *xxx*). However, the sys-unconfig utility reconfigures almost all system parameters, rather than just the hostname. Therefore, in some cases, it may be preferable to simply manually change the hostname. This can be done with the following script:

```
#/bin/sh
# Change the system hostname
# Usage:  newname <newhostname>
#
# Backup files and substitute new name in place
# of the old name
OLDNAME='uname -n'
echo "Changing hostname from $OLDNAME to $1"
for FILE in /etc/hosts        \
                /etc/nodename     \
                /etc/hostname.*l  \
                /etc/net/tic*/hosts ;
do
        cp $FILE $FILE.bak;
        echo "$FILE backed up as $FILE.bak"
        sed 's/$OLDNAME/$1/g' $FILE.bak > $FILE;
done
echo "Rebooting..."
/usr/sbin/reboot
```

Reconfiguring the System (sys-unconfig)

sys-
unconfig
1. Back up all files that will be changed:

   ■ cp /etc/hostname /etc/hostname.old

   ■ mkdir /etc/net.backup

   ■ cp /etc/net/* /etc/net.backup

   ■ cp /etc/nodename /etc/nodename.old

   ■ cp /etc/shadow /etc/shadow.old

   ■ chmod 600 /etc/shadow

   ■ cp /etc/TIMEZONE /etc/TIMEZONE.old

2. Reconfigure the system:

   ■ `/usr/sbin/sys-unconfig`

3. Reboot the system after it halts.

4. Answer configuration questions when prompted.

5. Wait while the system reboots.

Although it may be possible to change the hostname of a Solaris system by manually editing the required files, it is recommended that the `sys-unconfig` utility be used instead. Upon running `sys-unconfig`, the system will halt. The next time it is booted, the administrator will be prompted for configuration information. This utility will edit the following files when run:

File	Result
`/etc/hostname`	Remove the hostname.
`/etc/inet/hosts`	Copy the current hosts file to `/etc/inet/ hosts.saved` and replace it with the default hosts file.
`/etc/inet/netmasks`	Delete the file.
`/etc/net/*/hosts`	Remove all entries for local host.
`/etc/nodename`	Remove the hostname.
`/etc/shadow`	Remove the root password.
`/etc/TIMEZONE`	Reset the timezone to `PST8PDT`.

Along with the listed files, all NIS/NIS+ services are disabled. When complete, the system will be configured the same as a new "out-of-the-box" system.

This procedure cannot be used on diskless or dataless clients. If the hostname of a diskless or dataless client must be changed, manually edit the files listed above.

Editing the Message of the Day (MOTD)

The Message of the Day, or MOTD, is the system's message that is displayed to each user at login. The message is only displayed after the user has successfully logged in (supplying the correct username and password).

MOTD

The message is stored in a plain text file called /etc/motd that can be edited by the root user at any time. This can be done with any text editor (such as vi, pico, and so on). No rebooting is needed. The following is an example of an MOTD:

```
- - - - - - - - - - - - - - - - - - - - - - - - - - - - - - - - - - - - - - - -
Sun Microsystems Inc.   SunOS 5.5     Generic November 1995
- - - - - - - - - - - - - - - - - - - - - - - - - - - - - - - - - - - - - - - -
SYSTEM SHUTDOWN
System will be shutdown for maintenance on 10/12/98 from 8AM
until 11 AM.

Send questions to John Doe <doej@somehost.com>
- - - - - - - - - - - - - - - - - - - - - - - - - - - - - - - - - - - - - - - -
```

Modules

In previous versions of the SunOS operating system, the kernel had to be rebuilt to load or unload certain sections or modules. In Solaris 2.x, the modules are dynamically loaded and unloaded as needed. Therefore, there is no need to rebuild the kernel, and most times there is no need to manually configure/load modules at all. In spite of this, there may be a few occasions when a module must be unloaded manually to prevent problems. An example of this can sometimes be found when using the SunPC product from Sun Microsystems.

If, for some reason, a module must be manually manipulated, the following commands apply:

Command	Description
mod_info	Query a module.
mod_install	Install a module.
mod_remove	Remove a module.
modinfo	Display information about modules that are currently loaded.
modlinkage	Module linkage structure.
modload	Load a kernel module.

Modules can be forced to load upon boot by adding a forceload line to /etc/system. The general form of a forceload line is as follows:

    forceload: *modulename*

▶ **See Also** Kernel Parameters (102) for more information on editing /etc/system.

General Configuration

Adding a Device

Solaris automatically detects most hardware devices. When adding SCSI devices, the system must be rebooted. To do this, reboot to single-user mode first. Then reboot using the `boot -r` command. Make sure that all peripheral devices are turned on before booting the system. If booting from somewhere other than the default boot device, an alternate device can be specified by using the following:

    boot *device* -r

Alternatively, `/reconfigure` can be used, followed by a regular reboot. This accomplishes the same task. The advantage is that the reboot can be left unattended and the system should come back up properly on its own.

Adding a Device

Disabling Automounting of /home

1. Edit the `/etc/auto_master` file, commenting out the `/home` line by placing a `#` as the first character of the line.

2. Reload automount:

       /usr/sbin./automount

Solaris 2.x comes out-of-the-box with automounting enabled for use with NFS. By default, `automount` uses `/home` for home directories. This causes one of the most frequently experienced problems of new Solaris users. With automounting of `/home` enabled, no user home directories will be able to be written to the directory. To fix this, the `/home` directory is removed from automounter control.

Disabling Auto-mounting of /home

SunOS 4.x and SunOS 5.x Automounter Naming

In Solaris 1.x (including the SunOS 4.x series) the automounter files were called `auto.*` rather than `auto_*`. This is something to note when migrating systems from Solaris 1.x to Solaris 2.x. If, after an upgrade, there are automounting and NIS problems, check the filenames to make sure they have been properly changed to the new naming convention. The first file you should check is `auto_home`, making sure it is no longer called `auto.home`.

Changing the Console Terminal Type

The inittab file is read each time the system is booted. The line that controls the console setup starts with co: and is similar to the following:

```
co:234:respawn:/usr/lib/saf/ttymon -g -h -p "'uname -n'
console login: " -T sun -d /dev/console -l console -m
ldterm,ttcompat
```

The /usr/lib/saf/ttymon -T option controls the terminal type of the console, setting the TERM environment variable. To change the console terminal type, simply change the -T option parameter.

Changing the Root Login Shell

The root login shell is actually /sbin/sh. If the shell is not carefully changed, a mistake such as making the shell /usr/bin/tcsh can cause major problems. In some cases, /usr may not be mounted, leaving the root account with no shell to use. Therefore, always confirm that the root shell is statically linked and in the /sbin directory.

The root shell can be changed with the following command:

```
passwd -e shell root
```

Again, it is recommended that the root shell not be changed. An alternative approach would be to create a second account with the UID of 0 with an alternate shell. However, this too presents some security concerns.

A low-risk way of using a different shell when logging in to the system as root is to add a line to the .profile file that executes the desired shell. This can be done by adding the following lines to the .profile:

```
if [ -x /usr/bin/csh -a -r /.cshrc -a -n 'tty' ] ; then
              /usr/bin/csh;
              exit;
        fi
```

Kernel Tuning

Kernel Parameters

1. Edit the /etc/system file to reflect the desired changes.

2. Touch the reconfigure file:

```
touch /reconfigure
```

3. Reboot the system:

```
/usr/sbin/shutdown -i5
```

The kernel parameters are kept in /etc/system. This file is read once each time the system is booted. This is a plain text file that can be manually edited. There are few reasons why the /etc/system file should be changed. Some database and Java tools, however, do require modification of the system file.

The set command can be used to change parameters. These set commands are in the following form:

```
set parameter = value
```

Editable parameters are listed in the following table.

Parameter	Description
hires_tick	Set this to 1 to have a higher resolution system clock. Sets system Hz value to 1000.
hz	Manually set the clock resolution instead of using the hires_tick parameter. The value of this parameter must be an integer.
maxuprc	Maximum number of user processes.
maxusers	Maximum number of users.
nfssrv: nfs_portmon	NFS fileserver security. Set to 1 for increased security.
ngroups_max	Set the maximum number of groups per user. Default is 16.
noexec_user_ stack	*Solaris 2.6 only.* Set this parameter to 1 to prevent some simple forms of buffer overrun exploits.
noexec_user_ stack_log	*Solaris 2.6 only.* Set this parameter to 1 to log possible attempts to exploit the system using buffer overruns.
pt_cnt	Number of System V pseudo-terminals (ptys). Default is 48. Use boot -r after changing this instead of shutdown.
rlim_fd_cur	Set the soft limit on the maximum number of file descriptors. It is not recommended to increase this number past 256, and definitely not past 1024, when using Solaris 2.5 or earlier versions. This is not a problem in Solaris 2.6.
rlim_fd_max	Set hard limit on the maximum number of file descriptors.

continues >>

>>continued

Parameter	Description
rstchown	Set this parameter to 0 to allow all users to chown their own files. This is not recommended for security reasons.
sd:sd_max_ throttle	Maximum number of queued commands. Decreasing this to 10 may fix some SCSI/RAID problems.

Manually editing /etc/system is for experienced users only. It is possible to damage the system to the point that it will not boot. If this happens, halt the system and boot with the following:

```
boot -as
```

This will reconfigure the entire system. If prompted for a system filename, specify /dev/null or the name of the backed up /etc/system file.

6
Network
Administration

continues >>

Daemons and Servers

Internet Daemon (inetd)

inetd [*options*] [*config file*]   inetd

The Internet daemon controls all Internet services hosted by the system.
By default, inetd is started when the system is booted in any networked
run state. The daemon reads the configuration file at /etc/inetd.conf
when it is started. The Internet daemon is not usually manually started;
however, if it is, options can be used.

Option	Description
-d	Do not send inetd to background. The daemon is run in the foreground to provide debugging information.
-r n *interval*	Detect broken servers. If any service managed by inetd is started more than *n* times per *interval* seconds, it is considered broken and shut down for 10 minutes. After 10 minutes, the service is restarted. By default, inetd uses a behavior similar to -r40 60.
-s	Standalone. The daemon will not contact the service access controller (SAC) as it usually does.
-t	Trace all TCP service accesses using the syslog facility (daemon.notice priority). UDP services cannot be traced using this option.

UDP Services and nowait

Never set a UDP service to run as nowait. This will cause problems between
inetd and the UDP service, resulting in the spawning of multiple UDP
servers. Eventually the performance of the entire system will be adversely
affected.

The inetd daemon is configured using the /etc/inet/inetd.conf file.
There is a symbolic link to /etc/inetd.conf that has been provided for
BSD compatibility. The file is plain text and can be manually edited.
Send a HUP signal to the inetd process with the kill command.

To disable a service, it can be commented out by placing a # as the
first character of the line and restarting the inetd process.

The file has the following format:

```
service socket protocol wait-status uid program arguments
```

Field	Description
service	The name of the service as listed in the /etc/services file.
socket	Specify the type of socket:
	■ stream: stream
	■ dgram: datagram
	■ raw: raw
	■ seqpacket: sequenced packet
	■ tli: any transport layer interface endpoint
protocol	The protocol used for the service. It must be a protocol listed in the /etc/inet/protocols file. For RPC services, the protocol can be specified as rpc/*.
wait-status	Either wait or nowait. Most services use nowait except for datagram (UDP) services.
uid	Specify which user the daemon will run as. Most run as root.
program	Full path to the actual daemon program file.
arguments	Any arguments that are added to the program file command line. Only five arguments can be specified.

TCP Network Access Control Daemon (netacl)

netacl   netacl [-version] [-daemon port] service

Although the Internet Services daemon (inetd) provides the framework for configuring network services, it provides no means of controlling access to these services. inetd only provides individual services to *everyone* or to *no one*. In cases in which it is desirable to allow or deny access to individual network services to specific hosts, the TCP Network Access Control daemon (netacl) can be used. netacl is one component of the *TIS Firewall Toolkit* (fwtk), a collection of programs for enhancing the security of UNIX systems, written by Trusted Information Systems, Inc., and made available free of charge to anyone for non-commercial use (http://www.tis.com/research/software/fwtk).

netacl is invoked by inetd for each service for which access control is desired. netacl consults a configuration file (/usr/local/etc/netperm-table) to determine if the requested service is to be permitted to the requesting host, and if so, invokes the program configured to provide the service.

Option	Description
-version	Print netacl version information to the standard output (stdout) and exit.
-daemon *port*	Indicate that the netacl program should act as a daemon, listening for connection requests on the specified port, rather than being invoked by inetd. Port can be specified by name or number.
service	The mandatory service argument specifies a name by which an instance of netacl will identify its configuration file entries from those intended for other instances of netacl. This is customarily the same name as the program that netacl is to invoke to provide the service.

The configuration file /usr/local/etc/netperm-table is shared by all components of the TIS Firewall Toolkit. Configuration entries for netacl have the following format:

```
netacl-service: permit-hosts host-pattern [options args] -exec
➥program [args]

netacl-service: deny-hosts host-pattern
```

host-pattern is a hostname or IP address specification, which may include an asterisk (*) as a wildcard character. Additional configuration item options include the following:

Option	Description
-user *UID*	Specify a user ID under which netacl should invoke the specified program.
-group *GID*	Specify a group ID under which netacl should invoke the specified program.
-chroot *path*	Specify a path to which netacl should perform a chroot(2) before invoking the specified program.

Example

The /etc/inetd.conf entry

```
login stream tcp nowait root /usr/local/bin/netacl rlogind
```

accompanied by the /etc/inetd.conf entries

```
netacl-rlogind: permit-hosts 1.2.3.* -exec /usr/sbin/
➥in.rlogind
netacl-rlogind: deny-hosts *
```

results in the rlogin service being permitted to all hosts with IP addresses of the form 1.2.3.*, and being denied (and the attempt logged) for all others.

Network Listen Daemon (listen)

listen   /usr/lib/saf/listen [*options*]

The Listen daemon (listen) is part of the Service Access Facility (SAF). It listens on the network for requests for servers. After a request has been detected, the daemon will invoke a new instance of the appropriate server for each valid connection.

Option	Description
-m *prefix*	Use *prefix* as the prefix of the pathname.

Name Service Cache Daemon (nscd)

nscd   /usr/sbin/nscd [*options*]

The Name Service Cache daemon (nscd) maintains an internal database of the most commonly used DNS lookups. This daemon is used to cache information from the passwd, group, and hosts files. It will take up to ten seconds for the nscd to update its records after one of these files has been modified. Note that unlike these files, the /etc/nsswitch.conf file is not re-read after modification by nscd. If edited, ncsd must be restarted or the system must be rebooted. Commands can be passed to nscd by running it again on the command line. Any new options are passed to the currently running instance.

Restarting nscd

When the /etc/nsswitch.conf or /etc/nscd.conf files are modified, the name service cache daemon (nscd) must be restarted. This can be done by issuing the two following commands as the root user:

```
/etc/init.d/nscd stop
/etc/init.d/nscd start
```

Wait a few seconds for the nscd to properly exit before running the start command.

It should also be noted that the Name Service Cache daemon will continue to make network requests to refresh its internal database. This may cause problems when using asynchronous PPP (aspppd). To prevent this from occurring, set keep-hot-count to 0 in /etc/nscd.conf.

Option	Description
-e cache,yesno	Enable or disable the cache specified by cache. If yesno is yes, the cache is enabled. If it is no, the cache is disabled.
-f configfile	Use a configuration file other than the default. The configuration file is specified by configfile.
-g	Show current configuration.
-i cache	Invalidate the specified cache.

The Name Service Cache daemon is configured by editing the /etc/nscd.conf file. The file is parsed line by line. Comment lines begin with a # and are ignored. Valid cache names include hosts, passwd, and groups.

Configuration Attributes

Attribute	Description
check-files cachename yesno	Specify if the named cache should check its related files (such as the host file) for changes every ten seconds. If the value of yesno is yes it is enabled. If it is set to no, file checking is disabled.
debug-level level	Set the level and detail of debugging information provided. 0 provides the least detail and 10 provides the most. Setting this to a non-zero value will cause nscd to run in the foreground rather than in the background.
enable-cache cachename yesno	Specify if the named cache should be enabled. The value of yesno is either yes (enable) or no (disable).

continues >>

>>*continued*

Attribute	Description
keep-hot- ➥count ➥*cachename n*	Set the number of entries (*n*) to keep in the cache.
logfile *file*	Send debugging information to the specified file. The file can also be a special device such as /dev/tty (to send output to the console).
negative- ➥time-to-live ➥*chachename n*	Specify the time to live for unsuccessful queries. The time is specified by *n*, in seconds.
positive- ➥time-to-live ➥*cachename n*	Specify the time to live for successful queries. The time is specified by *n*, in seconds.
suggested- ➥size cachename ➥*size*	Sets the internal hash table size. The size should be a prime number.

NFS Daemon (nfsd)

nfsd   /usr/lib/nfs/nfsd [*options*] [*maxthreads*]

The NFS daemon controls requests for network filesystems via the NFS service. When nfsd is started automatically (in networked run states) it is run with the -a option, causing it to be started on both UDP and TCP transports. Optionally, an argument can be specified on the command line to limit the number of simultaneous connections (number of threads) to *maxthreads*.

Option	Description
-a	Start nfsd on both UDP and TCP transports.
-c *max*	Set the maximum number of connections (max) allowed to connect to the NFS server. By default, no limit is set.
-p *protocol*	Start the daemon only on the specified *protocol* (UDP or TCP).
-t *dev*	Run nfsd using the same transport as the specified device.

Network Lock Daemon (lockd)

/usr/lib/nfs/lockd [*options*]   lockd

The Network Lock daemon (lockd) is part of the NFS system. The daemon controls network file locking operations using the fcntl() and lockf() function calls. Any fcntl() calls that are received are forwarded to the lock manager on the appropriate NFS server. If the lockd daemon is killed while running state, information can be lost.

Option	Description
-g *graceperiod*	If the server is rebooted, the clients will have *graceperiod* seconds to reclaim locks.
-t *timeout*	Specify the time to wait (*timeout*, in seconds) before resending a lock request to an NFS server.

Network Router Discovery Daemon (in.rdisc)

/usr/sbin/in.rdisc   in.rdisc

The Network Router Discovery daemon (in.rdisc) populates the network routing tables when the system is booted by using the UCMP router discovery protocol. If the host is a non-routing host, in.rdisc listens on the ALL_HOSTS multicast address (224.0.0.1) for other routers. Routers of the highest priority (as set in their advertise messages) are accepted unless -a is specified on the command line. If the host is a routing host, the daemon will also alert other systems to the router present, sending out messages to the ALL_HOSTS multicast address every 600 seconds.

Option	Description
-a	Accept. Accept all routers that are discovered while listening on the ALL_HOSTS multicast address.
-f	Forever. Force the daemon to keep running even if no routers are discovered.
-p *pref*	When sending out messages to find routers, this option sets the preference (*pref*). By default, the value of *pref* is 0.

continues >>

>>continued

Option	Description
-r	Route. The daemon will behave as if it is running on a router rather than on a host.
-s	Send out three messages to attempt to find other routers. If none are found, the daemon will exit unless the -f option has been also specified.
-T *time*	Set the time between successive advertise messages. The default value is 600 seconds.

Network Routing Daemon (in.routed)

in.routed   /usr/sbin/in.routed [*options*]

The Network Routing daemon controls the system routing tables for network activity, listening on 520/udp for routing packets. If the host is a routing-host, the daemon will also provide copies of the routing tables to other hosts. As soon as the daemon is started it will look for configured network interfaces. If two interfaces are found, it assumes that packets are to be forwarded between the two interfaces (between the two networks). Network routing tables are updated as necessary. Unused entries are deleted about every four minutes. The files /etc/gateways and /etc/networks are used for configuration purposes.

Option	Description
-g	Gateway. Used on hosts acting as routers to provide a default route.
-q	Do not supply routing information.
-s	Supply routing information. This information is supplied whether or not the host is a router.
-S	Enter only default routes for internetwork routing (if acting as an internetwork router).
-t	Trace. Print all packets received on standard output.

Network Finger Daemon (in.fingerd)

in.fingerd   /usr/sbin/in.fingerd

The Network Finger daemon handles requests for finger information on port 79/tcp. Finger requests sent to the Finger daemon are actually passed to the finger command on the server host to generate a reply.

Note that, by default, finger requests are not logged and can give out information to potential system intruders. The Finger daemon should be run only if truly necessary, as it is a security concern. To disable the Finger daemon, comment out the appropriate line in the /etc/inetd.conf file.

▶ **See Also** Internet Daemon (inetd) (107).

Network Wall Daemon (rwalld)

/usr/lib/netsvc/rwall/rpc.walld   rwalld

The Network Wall daemon (rwalld) processes requests from the rwall command (see rwall). The daemon takes the request and passes it to the wall command on all network machines. This daemon is not necessary and disabling it should be considered. It will keep users from broadcasting unnecessary messages to every machine on the network. To disable it, comment out the walld line in /etc/inetd.conf and restart the inetd process.

▶ **See Also** rwall (88)

Boot Parameter Server (rpc.bootparamd)

/usr/sbin/rpc.bootparamd [*options*]   rpc.
                                                                  bootparamd

The Boot Parameter server (also known as a BOOTP server), rpc.
bootparamd, is used to pass boot parameters to diskless clients on the network. The daemon must be running on the same IP subnet as the diskless client. Boot parameters are defined in the /etc/nsswitch.conf and /etc/bootparams files.

Option	Description
-d	Show debugging information.

The /etc/bootparams file has the following format:

hostname id

The first field (*hostname*) is the hostname of the diskless client. This field can be a specific hostname of a client, or a wildcard (*) can be used to represent all clients. If the wildcard is specified and individual clients are specified, the client-specific lines will override the wildcard lines. As in the case of most Solaris configuration files, long lines can be split using a backslash (\) to break the line.

The second field (*id*) is the identification field. It can be of either of the following forms:

```
File-specific: id=host:path

Non-file-specific: id=domain
```

File-specific configuration IDs will instruct the diskless client to use the exported file or filesystem on the named host. The host and the pathname to the file or filesystem must be separated by a colon. The non–file-specific configuration ID assigns a domain name to the client. If a domain name is specified after the equal sign, it is used. If none is specified, the server's domain name is used. The only IDs that can be used for SPARC diskless clients are root, swap, and dump.

The final type of entry is the name service configuration line. It has the following format:

```
ns=[nameserver]:[nameservice]:[(netmask)]
```

The name server is specified in the first field, *nameserver*. The second field can be one of three name service types: nis, nisplus, or none. The last field is the netmask for the client. Netmasks are used to specify which part of an IP address is a network address and which part is the host address. For an IP address of 192.168.0.4 with a netmask of 255.255.255.0, the 4 in the IP is the host address.

By default, NIS+ is used as the naming service if a NIS+ server is found. Otherwise, a NIS server will be used if found. If no name service is found, an interactive screen will be displayed on the client asking for which name service to use. The following is an example of an /etc/bootparams file.

```
*     root=fs1:/export/cslab/root
ice9 root=fs1:/export/ice9/root
      swap=fs1:/export/ice9/swap
      domain=cslab.somecollege.edu
      ns=mach:nis(255.255.255.0)
```

RPC Remote Execution Daemon (rpc.rexd)

rpc.rexd   /usr/sbin/rpc.rexd [*options*]

The Remote Execution daemon (rpc.rexd) handles remote program execution requests from the network. The on program is a zclient. Non-interactive programs run via remote execution are run in a manner similar to rsh.

Interactive programs will have a pseudo-terminal assigned so that the session will behave similarly to an rlogin session. This daemon can be a security hazard and should only be run if absolutely necessary. Diagnostic messages from the daemon are usually sent to the console.

Option	Description
-s	Secure. Any remote execution request must have valid DES encryption credentials in order to be processed. Authentication is set using the chkey command.

Telnet Daemon (in.telnetd)
/usr/sbin/in.telnetd   in.telnetd

The telnet daemon (in.telnetd) allows remote users to log in to the system and work via a pseudo-terminal. The daemon listens on port 23/tcp for connections. Environment variables can be passed via the telnet daemon during the initial terminal negotiation. This ability is commonly used to pass a DISPLAY variable to use OpenWindows.

Talk Daemon (in.talkd)
/usr/sbin/in.talkd   in.talkd

The Talk daemon (in.talkd) is used to communicate using the talk program, listening for requests on port 514/udp. Although talkd listens on a UDP port, after the connection has been established, the chatting via the talk programs is accomplished via the TCP protocol.

▶ **See Also** talk (88)

Remote Shell Daemon (in.rshd)
/usr/sbin/in.rshd   in.rshd

The Remote Shell daemon (rshd) handles command execution requests from the rsh command. Access depends on the /etc/hosts.equiv and user .rhosts files. This system uses a host/username-based authentication system. However, if Kerberos is used, there is no need to use the .rhosts files, provided a higher degree of security.

▶ **See Also** rlogin (90), Kerberos (222)

System Status Daemon (in.rwhod)

in.rwhod   /usr/sbin/in.rwhod [*options*]

The System Status daemon (sometimes called the rwho daemon),
in.rwhod, handles requests from the rwho and ruptime client programs.
The daemon gathers information about the local system and sends it out as
a broadcast/multicast for other rwho daemons to pick up off the network.
Also, it listens for information coming from other daemons, recording it in
the /var/spool/rwho directory.

Daemon Can Cause Excessive Network Traffic

Each System Status daemon on the network constantly sends out system
information to other rwho daemons. If only a few hosts are running these
daemons on a network, this is not a problem. However, if a large number
of hosts are running these daemons, the daemon activity can substantially
increase the amount of network traffic, causing possible slowing of the
network. For this reason, and for security reasons, this daemon should only
be used if absolutely necessary.

Option	Description
-m	Use the multicast address (224.0.1.3) when sending out system information to other rwho daemons. The daemon will multicast on all interfaces but will not be forwarded by multicast routers.

File Transfer Protocol Daemon (in.ftpd)

in.ftpd   /usr/sbin/in.ftpd [*options*]

The File Transfer Protocol (FTP) daemon (ftpd) handles file transfer
requests sent by ftp clients. The daemon is run via the inetd service. By
default, only users with accounts on the system (valid usernames and
passwords) can FTP to the system. If the user's username is listed in
/etc/ftpusers, access will be denied. However, it is possible to set up
"anonymous FTP" that will allow any user with access to the system to
perform file transfers in restricted directories.

User Shells Must Be in /etc/shells

One common problem that exists on Solaris systems is that if a user is using
a non-standard command shell (such as tcsh or zsh), he will not be able to
FTP to the host. To fix this problem, add the user's shell to the /etc/shells
file. The full path must be specified.

If the /etc/shells file does not exist, the default shells that are allowed are as follows:

```
/bin/csh      /bin/jsh      /bin/ksh
/bin/sh       /sbin/jsh     /sbin/sh
/usr/bin/csh  /usr/bin/jsh  /usr/bin/ksh
/usr/bin/sh
```

Option	Description
-d	Debug. Extra information is logged using the syslog facility.
-l	Log each access of the FTP daemon to the syslog facility. This is highly recommended as a security precaution.
-t *timeout*	Specify the amount of inactivity (in seconds) before the daemon disconnects.

Supported Operations

Operation	Description
ABOR	Abort.
ACCT	Set account.
ALLO	Allocate storage.
APPE	Append to file.
CDUP	Change the current working directory to the parent directory.
CWD	Change working directory.
DELE	Delete.
HELP	Print command summary.
LIST	List files (same as ls -gl).
MKD	Make directory.
MODE	Set mode of transfer.
NLST	List files and directories (same as ls).
NOOP	No operation (do nothing).
PASS	Password.
PASV	Passive mode.
PORT	Set port.

continues >>

>>continued

Operation	Description
PWD	Print working directory.
QUIT	Exit.
RETR	Get a file.
RMD	Delete a directory.
RNFR	Rename from.
RNTO	Rename to.
STOR	Store.
STOU	Store (unique name).
STRU	Structure.
TYPE	Type of data transfer.
USER	Username.
XCUP	Change current working directory to the parent of the current directory.
XCWD	Change working directory.
XMKD	Make directory.
XPWD	Print working directory.
XRMD	Remove directory.

Domain Name Server (in.named)

in.named   `/usr/sbin/in.named [options]`

The Domain Name server provides domain name service (DNS) to clients on the network. By default, the daemon uses the file `/etc/named.boot` to gather initial DNS information. A separate utility called `named-xfer` is used by the daemon to perform zone transfers. This utility should not be run manually at any time. The daemon can be forced to reread the `named.boot` file by sending a `SIGHUP` (`kill -HUP daemonpid`) to the daemon.

Getting DNS to Work

By default, Solaris systems are set to use only local files for DNS lookups. To allow Internet lookups using a DNS server, the `/etc/nsswitch.conf` file must be edited. Locate the following line in the file:

```
hosts: files
```

Edit it to read as follows:

```
hosts: files dns
```

This will cause lookups to be first attempted using the /etc/hosts file and then by using the DNS nameserver specified in the /etc/resolv.conf file.

Option	Description
-b *file*	Rather than using /etc/named.boot, use the file specified by *file*.
-d *level*	Debug. Extra information is printed for debugging purposes. The higher the level, the more detail is given.
-p *port*	Specify a port to listen on.

The configuration file /etc/named.boot supports the following types of entries:

Entry	Description
domain *domain*	The DNS domain. No leading dot is needed.
primary *domain file*	Specifies that the domain information for *domain* is located in the file *file*. The file is usually named.db.
secondary *domain* ↦*server1 server2 ....*	Specifies one or more secondary servers to gather DNS information about *domain*.
cache *file*	Specifies what database file is to be placed in the cache.

The ./etc/resolv.conf file is used to configure how hostnames are resolved on the local host. The file is plain text and can be edited manually. The file can contain the following types of entries:

Entry	Description
nameserver *addr*	Specifies the nameserver (DNS server) that the system should use to look up Internet names. More than one nameserver can be specified by adding additional nameserver *addr* lines. This way, backup servers can be listed.
domain *name*	Default domain name to append to hostnames if no domain name is given.

Remote Login Daemon (in.rlogind)

in.rlogind   /usr/sbin/in.rlogind

The Remote Login daemon (called the rlogin daemon) handles remote login requests from the rlogin program. The daemon listens on port 514/tcp. Authentication and access is based on a hostname/username-based system. This system uses .rhosts files as well as /etc/hosts.equiv. If the Kerberos system is used, these files are not necessary and authentication is based on Kerberos tickets. Also, the client's source port must be in the range of 0–1023 or it will be denied access to the system. If all security checks are passed, a pseudo-terminal is created and the user is allowed to log in.

The rlogin and rsh systems are not very secure. The rlogind and rshd daemons should be used only on very trusted networks. It is recommended that they not be used at all unless absolutely necessary.

Network Username Daemon (rusersd)

rusersd   /usr/lib/netsvc/rusers/rpc.rusersd

The Network Username daemon (ruser daemon) responds to requests from the rusers command. The daemon is started when either the Listen daemon or inetd receive a request that was broadcast on the network.

Kernel Statistics Daemon (rstatd)

rstatd   /usr/lib/netsvc/rstat/rpc.rstatd

The Kernel Statistics daemon (rstatd) responds to requests sent by the rup utility. The statistics are pulled from the kernel and sent out over the network. Unless a specific need for this daemon can be determined, it should be disabled for security reasons.

Network Spray Daemon (sprayd)

sprayd   /usr/lib/netsvc/spray/rpc.sprayd

The Network Spray daemon (sprayd daemon) responds to packets sent by the spray utility. The service works similarly to pinging a system to find a response time and number of dropped packets. However, the Spray daemon can be unreliable at times, causing packets to be incorrectly reported as dropped.

Network Status Daemon (statd)

/usr/lib/nfs/statd   statd

The Network Status daemon is used by the NFS facility, along with the
Lock daemon, to prevent and recover from crashes. The Status daemon
does this by alerting other systems that the host has been successfully
rebooted after a crash. After the other systems have been alerted, an
attempt can be made to reclaim any locks and continue operation.

File	Description
/var/statmon/ sm	File containing hosts that should be contacted after a crash and reboot.
/var/statmon/ sm.bak	A list generated by the daemon of hosts that could not be contacted after the last crash.
/var/statmon/ state	A file containing a single number that denotes the system status.

Network File System (NFS)

Mounted Filesystem Table

/etc/mnttab   Mounted
                                                                              Filesystem
                                                                              Table
The mounted filesystem table (called the mount-tab file), /etc/mnttab,
contains information of all mounted filesystems. The mount command adds
entries to this file (unless the -m option is used). The umount command
removes entries from this file. The file has the following format:

special mount_point fstype options time

NFS mounted filesystem resource names are in *host:resource* format
and are marked nfs in the *fstype* field.

Field	Description
special	Resource name.
mount_point	Resource mount point.
fstype	Filesystem type.
options	Mount options.
time	Mount time.

Example

The following is an example of a working /etc/mnttab file. Both UFS and NFS filesystems are shown. In this example, NFS filesystems have been mounted on host11 and host22.

```
/dev/dsk/c0t3d0s0        /       ufs      rw,suid,dev=800018
➡905203176
/dev/dsk/c0t2d0s6        /usr    ufs      rw,suid,dev=800016
➡905203176
/proc     /proc    proc   rw,suid,dev=2700000  905203176
fd        /dev/fd fd      rw,suid,dev=2780000  905203176
/dev/dsk/c0t3d0s3        /var    ufs      rw,suid,dev=80001b
➡905203176
/dev/dsk/c0t2d0s5        /tmp    ufs      suid,rw,dev=800015
➡905203178
/dev/dsk/c0t2d0s7        /var/tmp         ufs
➡suid,rw,dev=800017    905203179
/dev/dsk/c1t2d0s1        /var/spool/news ufs
➡suid,rw,dev=800089    905203179
/dev/dsk/c1t1d0s6        /home   ufs      suid,rw,dev=800086
➡905203178
/dev/dsk/c1t1d0s7        /home/ouser      ufs
➡suid,rw,dev=800087    905203179
/dev/dsk/c0t0d0s6        /home/suser      ufs
➡suid,rw,quota,dev=800006    905203179
/dev/dsk/c0t0d0s7        /home/host22     ufs
➡suid,rw,dev=800007    905203179
-hosts    /net     autofs  ignore,indirect,nosuid,dev=2880001
➡905203222
-xfn      /xfn     autofs  ignore,indirect,dev=2880002  905203222
host11:vold(pid209)      /vol    nfs
➡ignore,noquota,dev=2840001 905203244
host22:/usr/local        /usr/local       nfs   soft,dev=2840002
➡905203257
host22:/opt    /opt     nfs     soft,dev=2840003       905203257
host22:/usr/share/man    /usr/share/man  nfs   soft,dev=2840004
➡905203257
host22:/usr/X11R6.1      /usr/X11R6.1     nfs   soft,dev=2840005
➡905203257
```

Sharing/Exporting NFS Resources

Sharing/
Exporting
NFS
Resources

/usr/bin/share [*options*] [*pathname*]

The share command is used to export NFS filesystems to other computers. If no pathname to export is specified, the command will display all filesystems that are currently exported.

Option	Description
-F *type*	Specify the filesystem type. If this option is not used, the first type listed in `./etc/dfs/fstypes` is used.
-o *options*	Specify filesystem-specific options that can be used. Options should be in the form of a comma-delimited list.
-d *descrip*	Add a description of the shared resource. The description is set to the string *descrip*.

Options for Sharing NFS Filesystems

Option	Description
aclok	If this option is specified, every user accessing the shared resource has the rights of the most unrestricted user. This will severely decrease the amount of security provided. Care should be taken when using this option.
anon=*uid*	Set the effective UID of unauthenticated users to that specified by *uid*. If *uid* is set to -1, all unauthenticated users will be denied access. Default behavior is to set the effective *uid* to that of the "nobody" user.
kerberos	Only Kerberos will be accepted as a valid method of authentication. Unauthenticated users will be treated as specified by the anon option.
nosub	No subdirectories may be mounted in shared directories. This option increases the security of the shared filesystems.
nosuid	If this option is set, users will not be allowed to create setuid or setgid files.
ro	Read-only.
ro=*host:host2* *:host3*.....	Set access to read-only for specified clients. Hosts are listed in a colon-delimited list after the equal sign (=).
root=*host: host2: host3*.....	Root access can only be achieved from the listed hostnames. Hosts are listed in a colon-delimited list after the equal sign (=).
rw	Read-write access.

continues >>

>>continued

Option	Description
rw=*host:host2:* *host3....*	Set access to read–write for the listed hosts. Hosts are listed in a colon–delimited list after the equals sign (=).
secure	Secure mode. All clients must use DES authentication. Unauthenticated users will be treated as defined by the anon option.

File	Description
/etc/dfs/ dfstab	Commands to be executed when the system is booted.
/etc/dfs/ fstypes	Identify the default filesystem type (NFS), as well as all other filesystem types.
/etc/dfs/ sharetab	Table of all shared resources.

Unshare an NFS Resource

Unshare an
NFS
Resource

```
/usr/bin/unshare [options] [pathname]
/usr/bin/unshareall
```

Remove a shared resource from /etc/sharetab so that it is no longer exported as an NFS filesystem. To get a list of what filesystems are shared, use the share command with no options. The unshareall command will unshare all currently shared filesystems.

Option	Description
-F *type*	Specify a filesystem type. By default, NFS is used. Other valid types are listed in the ./etc/dfs/fstypes file.
-o	Specify other filesystem-specific options.

Display NFS Statistics

Display NFS
Statistics

```
/usr/bin/nfsstat [options]
```

Statistical information concerning the NFS system can be retrieved using the nfsstat utility. The utility directly pulls information from the kernel of the local host. If used with the -z option by the root user, statistics can be reset with this command as well. The default behavior (no options) is the same as nfsstat -cnrs.

Option	Description
-c	Client information. Client-side NFS and RPC information is summarized and displayed.
-m	Show extra information for each mounted filesystem, including the following: ■ Mount flags ■ Read/write sizes ■ Resend count ■ Round trip time ■ Server address ■ Server name ■ Timers
-n	NFS client and server information. Both client and server information for NFS is summarized and printed.
-r	Display only RPC information.
-s	Display only server information.
-z	Zero stats. Reset all statistics back to zero and start over. This option can be used only by the root user.

Display Fields

Field	Description
badcalls	Number of calls rejected
badlen	Number of calls that were too short
badverfs	Number of bad verifiers
badxids	Number of bad received calls
calls	Number of calls (NFS or RPC, depending on options) received
cantconn	Number of times a connection could not be made to the server
clgets	Number of received client handles
cltoomany	Number of times cache had no unused entries

continues >>

>>continued

Field	Description
dupchecks	Number of duplicate request cache lookups
dupreqs	Number of duplicates found
interrupts	Number of interrupts received
newcreds	Number of authentication refreshes
nomem	Number of times a call failed due to lack of memory
nullrecv	Number of times an unavailable call was reported as received
retrans	Number of times a call was resent
timeouts	Number of timed-out calls
timers	Number of inconsistent timeout values
xdrcall	Number of calls with bad XDR headers

Example

To print only server NFS information, use the following utility and options:

```
nfsstat -ns
```

Mounting and Unmounting NFS Filesystems

Mounting and Unmounting NFS Filesystems

The mount and umount commands are used to mount and unmount filesystems, respectively. Mounting a filesystem attaches it to the existing filesystem hierarchy so that it can be used. A table of mounted filesystems is kept in the mnttab (pronounced mount-tab) file at /etc/mnttab.

Options Used with All Filesystem Types

Option	Description
-a	Mount all filesystems specified in /etc/vfstab as "mount at boot" in parallel if possible. If the umount command is being used, all filesystems listed in /etc/mnttab are unmounted.
-a mountpoints	If the umount command is being used, only the mount points listed are unmounted.
-F type	Specify the type of filesystem to mount.
-m	Mount filesystem without adding an entry to /etc/mnttab.

continues >>

Option	Description
-o	Specify filesystem-specific mount options. Options should be separated by commas.
-O	Overlay. The filesystem is mounted over a currently mounted mount point. The underlying filesystem will not be usable after this operation.
-p	Print the filesystems in /etc/vfstab. No other options can be used with this option.
-r	Mount the filesystem as read-only.
-v	Print the filesystems in /etc/vfstab showing all information (verbose). No other options can be used with this option.
-V	Print the command line, but do not execute anything.

Options Used with NFS Filesystems

Option	Description
acdirmax=n	Do not cache attributes for more than n seconds after update.
acdirmin=n	Cache attributes for at least n seconds after directory update.
acregmax=n	Do not cache attributes for more than n seconds after file modification.
acregmin=n	Cache attributes after file modification for at least n seconds.
actimeo=n	Set both min and max times for files and directories. The times are set to n, in seconds.
bg	Background mount if first mount attempt is not successful.
fg	Foreground mount.
grpid	Set newly created directory group ownerships to that of the parent directory.
hard	Continue to retry even if server does not respond initially.
intr	Allow keyboard interrupts to halt processes that are hung due to NFS.
kerberos	Require Kerberos authentication.
noac	Do not cache data or attributes.

continues >>

>>continued

Option	Description
nointr	Do not allow keyboard interrupts to halt processes that are hung due to NFS. The default is to allow interrupts.
noquota	Disable quotas.
nosuid	setuid execution is not allowed.
port=n	Set the NFS server port number.
posix	Use POSIX.1 semantics.
proto=netid	Set the protocol transport by network ID from /etc/netconfig.
quota	Enable quotas.
remount	Remount filesystem from ro to rw.
retrans=n	Set number of retransmissions.
retry=n	Number of times to retry on failure.
ro	Read-only access allowed.
rsize=n	Set buffer size to n bytes. The default value is 32,768 bytes.
rw	Read-write access allowed.
secure	NFS requires the use of DES authentication.
soft	Return an error if the server does not respond.
suid	setuid execution allowed.
timeo=n	Set timeout to n in tenths of a second. Default is 11.
vers=n	Set the NFS version number.
wsize=n	Set write buffer size to n bytes.

Examples

Mount a filesystem on nserv1 on the local machine as /usr/foo:

```
mount nserv1:/usr/export/foo /usr/foo
```

Mount the same filesystem, but as read-only:

```
mount -ro nserv1:/usr/export/foo /usr/foo
```

Manually mount the remote ufs filesystem /data from host tokyo to the directory /data on the local system:

```
mkdir -p /data
mount -F nfs tokyo:/data /data
```

Or, to have the filesystem automatically mounted each time the system is rebooted, add the following line to the file /etc/vfstab:

```
tokyo:/data - /data nfs - yes -
```

Then type the following:

```
mkdir -p /data
mountall
```

Manually mount the remote hsfs filesystem /cdrom from host tokyo, read-only, to the directory /net/tokyo/cdrom on the local system:

```
mkdir -p /net/tokyo/cdrom
mount -F nfs -r tokyo:/cdrom /net/tokyo/cdrom
```

Or, to have the filesystem automatically mounted each time the system is rebooted, add the following line to the file /etc/vfstab:

```
tokyo:/cdrom - /net/tokyo/cdrom nfs - yes ro
```

Then type the following:

```
mkdir -p /net/tokyo/cdrom
mountall
```

Use the automounter to automatically mount the remote filesystem /usr/man from any of the hosts tokyo, boston, or rio to the directory /usr/man on the local system, each time an attempt is made to access the /usr/man directory.

Add the following line to the file /etc/auto_master:

```
/- auto_direct
```

Add the following line to the file /etc/auto_direct:

```
/usr/man tokyo,boston,rio:/usr/man
```

Then type the following:

```
mkdir -p /usr/man
automount
```

Mail

The sendmail Daemon

The sendmail
Daemon

`/usr/lib/sendmail [options] [address]`

The `sendmail` daemon routes email for both the local host as well as Internet email. In most cases, `sendmail` is not used manually, and is instead called by other programs. However, `sendmail` can be used from the command line to send mail. If no options are specified, the daemon will read data from standard input until an EOF or a line with a single dot is reached. If the address given is a single username, it is assumed to be a user on the local system. If the address is of the format *user@host.com*, it is assumed to be Internet email and will be routed accordingly. Undeliverable mail will be sent back to the sender (known as "bouncing the message").

Option	Description
-B *type*	Body type: 7BIT or 8BITMIIME.
-ba	ARPANET mode. All lines of input must be terminated with a return-linefeed. Both the From: and Sender: fields are checked for the address of the sender.
-bd	Run as a daemon.
-bi	Initialize the aliases database.
-bm	Default method of mail delivery.
-bp	Print mail queue summary.
-bt	Test mode. Parsing steps for addresses are shown.
-bv	Do not deliver the message—verify only.
-C *file*	Specify a configuration file other than the default.
-d *n*	Set debugging level to *n*.
-F *fullname*	Set the sender's full name.
-f *name*	Set the From: field of the mail. Only trusted users can use this option.
-h *n*	Set hop count to *n* hops. Mail will be bounced after *n* hops.
-M *id*	Mail the message with mail-id of *id*.
-n	No aliases.

continues >>

Option	Description
-o *a value*	Processing option. *a* is the option and *value* is the value. For a list of common options, see the next section, "sendmail Configuration."
-p *protocol*	Define the protocol for sending mail.
-q	Process the mail queue. If a time is specified, the mail queue is processed on a regular basis. The time is specified as a number and units. Valid units are as follows: ■ s: seconds ■ m: minutes ■ h: hours ■ d: days ■ w: weeks
-R *string*	Attempt to send any queued mail with a recipient matching the specified string.
-t	Scan messages for To:, Cc:, and Bcc: fields to determine recipients.
-v	Verbose. Extra information will be given, including alias expansions.
-X *log*	Log all sendmail uses in the specified log file.

sendmail Configuration

/usr/lib/sendmail.cf

sendmail
Configuration

The sendmail daemon can be configured by editing the sendmail.cf file. A full reference for the administration of sendmail is beyond the scope of this text. Some of the basic configuration options have been listed below. Individual options can also be specified on the sendmail command line using the -o option.

Basic Configuration Options

Option	Description
7	Force input to be stripped to 7-BIT to comply with old systems.

continues >>

>>continued

Option	Description
A *file*	Specify an alias file.
a *n*	Wait *n* minutes for an @:@ entry in the mail aliases database before starting.
B *c*	Set black substitution character to *c*.
b *n/m w*	Only send mail if at least *n* blocks are free on the mail queue filesystem. A maximum mail size can also be set by adding the /m, where *w* is the size.
C *n*	Checkpoint large mail queues every *n* addresses. The default value is 10.
D	Rebuild the aliases database.
d *mode*	Delivery mode: ■ i: Interactive ■ b: Background ■ q: Queue and do not send
E /*file*	Preface all mailed error messages with the file containing a message.
e *mode*	Handle errors in mode: ■ p: Print errors. ■ q: Quiet, no messages. ■ m: Mail errors. ■ w: Use write to send errors. ■ e: Mail errors and force zero return value.
f	Save from headers (UNIX style).
F *mode*	File mode.
g *n*	Set group ID to *n*.
H *file*	Set the help file for the SMTP daemon.
h *n*	Set max hop count to *n*.
i	Ignore dots.
I	Nameserver must be running to send mail.
j	Send error messages in MIME format.

continues >>

Option	Description
J *path*	Forward file (.forward) search path. Set to *user*/.forward.
k *n*	Set the maximum number of connections to *n*.
K *time*	Maximum time to allow a cached and inactive connection to live.
l	Use Errors-To: header.
L *n*	Set logging level. Default value is 9.
M *m val*	Set the macro (*m*) to some value (*val*).
n	When the aliases database is rebuilt, also validate the RHS of addresses.
o	Treat headers as if they are old format.
O *opt*	SMTP server options as *key=value* pairs: ■ Port=*n*: Set port number. ■ Addr=*n*: Set address mask. ■ Family=*n*: Set address family. ■ Listen=*n*: Set size of listen queue.
p *opt,opt,...*	Privacy Options: ■ public: No privacy ■ needmailhelo: Require a HELO or EHLO. ■ needexpnhelo: Require a HELO or EHLO before an EXPN command. ■ noexpn: Disallow EXPN commands. ■ needvrfyhelo: Require a HELO or EHLO before a VRFY command. ■ novrfy: Disallow VRFY. ■ restrictmailq: Restrict access to the mailq command. ■ restrictqrun: Restrict access to the -q option for sendmail command lines. ■ authwarnings: Use X-Authentication. ■ Warning: headers.
P *pmaster*	Define a postmaster to send copies of error messages to.

continues >>

>>continued

Option	Description
Q *dir*	Specify a different queue directory.
q *n*	Set map function multiplier to *n*, when deciding when to queue and when to run jobs. Default value is `600000`.
s	Super-Safe. The queue file is always instantiated.
S *file*	Statistics are to be logged to the specified file.
T *rt/wt*	Set the timeout after which mail is bounced (`rt`) and after which a warning is sent (`wt`). Default bounce time is five days.
t *TZ*	Set the timezone to *TZ*.
u *n*	Set the default mailer user identification number (`uid`) to *n*.
v	Verbose. Extra detail is provided displaying all mail delivery steps.
V *fbh*	Define a fall-back-host. If no other mail exchange host works, the fall-back-host is used.
x *load*	If the system average load is greater than *load*, messages are queued and not sent.
X *load*	If the system average load is greater than *load*, no more SMTP connections are allowed.
Y	Save memory by sending each queued message in a separate process.
y *n*	Lower the priority of jobs with many recipients. The default value is 30000.

SMTP Application Proxy (smap)

smap   smap [-*daemon port*]

On systems that are not protected from electronic attack from untrustworthy users through the use of a network firewall, it may be deemed desirable to use a secure proxy application to avoid allowing remote systems to communicate directly with the sendmail program. In such cases, the SMTP Application Proxy (smap) can be used. smap is one component of the TIS Firewall Toolkit (fwtk), a collection of programs for enhancing the security of UNIX systems, written by Trusted Information Systems, Inc., and made available free of charge to anyone for non-commercial use.

smap can either be run as a daemon listening for connection requests on the specified port (by default, smap uses the standard SMTP port 25), or it can be invoked by inetd for each SMTP connection request received. smap consults a configuration file (/usr/local/etc/netperm-table) to determine the directory to make its root directory and to determine the user and group IDs to set itself to before accepting the SMTP connection with the remote system. smap then receives mail from the remote system, placing the mail in a spool directory within its restricted environment, which is then scanned periodically (by default, every 60 seconds) by the SMTP Proxy Server (smapd), which invokes the sendmail program to route or deliver each message. In this way, the remote system is prevented from communicating directly with the sendmail program, which must necessarily run with root privileges in an unrestricted environment.

Option	Description
-daemon port	Indicate that the smap program should act as a daemon, listening for connection requests on the specified port, rather than being invoked by inetd. *port* can be specified by name or number.

The configuration file /usr/local/etc/netperm-table is shared by all components of the TIS Firewall Toolkit. Configuration entries for smap have the following format:

    smap: *option*

where *option* includes the following:

Option	Description
userid *name*	Specify the user name or UID under which smap should communicate with the remote system.
groupid *name*	Specify the group name or GID under which smap should communicate with the remote system.
directory *path*	Specify the path to which smap should perform a chroot(2) before communicating with the remote system.
timeout *seconds*	Specify the number of seconds smap will keep an idle connection open before disconnecting from the remote system.

Example

The /etc/inetd.conf entry

```
smtp stream tcp nowait root /usr/local/bin/smap smap
```

accompanied by the /usr/local/etc/netperm-table entries

```
smap: userid noaccess
smap: groupid NOACCESS
smap: directory /var/spool/smap
```

results in the smap program communicating with remote systems with the privileges of user and group noaccess and with the directory /var/spool/smap as its root directory.

smapd

smapd   smapd [*option*]

---

smapd is started when the system boots and runs as a daemon, scanning the smap spool directory periodically and invoking sendmail to deliver the mail messages it finds in the spool directory.

Option	Description
-d	Indicate that the smapd program should display status messages as it processes the mail messages in the spool directory.

smapd reads configuration entries from the file /usr/local/etc/netperm-table. Configuration entries for smapd have the following format:

```
smapd: option
```

where *option* includes the following:

Option	Description
userid *name*	Specify the user name or UID under which smapd should run.
groupid *name*	Specify the group name or GID under which smapd should run.
directory *path*	Specify the path to which smap should perform a chroot(2) before invoking the mail delivery program.
baddir *path*	Specify the directory into which smapd will place mail that it cannot deliver.

continues >>

Option	Description
wakeup *seconds*	Specify the number of seconds smapd will sleep between scans of the spool directory.
executable *prog*	Specify the program name that the smapd program will use to fork a copy of itself.
sendmail *prog*	Specify the name of the program smapd will invoke to deliver the mail messages read from the spool directory.
maxchildren *n*	Specify the maximum number of processes smapd will spawn concurrently to deliver the mail messages read from the spool directory.

Example

The /usr/local/etc/netperm-table entries:

```
smapd: userid noaccess
smapd: groupid noaccess
smapd: directory /var/spool/smap
smapd: baddir /var/spool/smap/undelivered
smapd: executable /usr/local/bin/smapd
smapd: sendmail /usr/lib/sendmail
smapd: maxchildren 5
```

result in the smapd program running with the privileges of user and group noaccess, scanning the directory /var/spool/smap for mail every 60 seconds (the default), forking a maximum of five concurrent instances of itself, each of which invokes the /usr/lib/sendmail program to deliver the mail, and placing undeliverable messages in the directory /var/spool/smap/undelivered.

7
Startup and Shutdown

Power Management

Power Management Daemon (powerd)

`/usr/lib/power/powed` [*options*]

Two types of shutdowns utilize the Solaris Power Management daemon (powerd). These are automatic shutdowns and low–power shutdowns.

Automatic shutdowns can occur if the current time is within the time limits specified under `autoshutdown` in the `/etc/power.conf` file and if the system has been idle for at least as long as specified in the same line in the `configuration` file.

Low-power shutdowns are used by battery-operated systems and are not an issue for most Solaris systems. If the daemon detects that the battery charge is too low, the system will perform an orderly shutdown before the battery gives out. In all cases, a warning message is sent to the `syslog` facility before shutting down.

The daemon is configured using the `/etc/power.conf` file and the `pmconfig` utility. The daemon can be forced to reload this configuration file by sending a HUP signal to the `powerd` process (`kill -HUP` *powerd-pid*).

Never place a piece of hardware under power management that is not designed for it.

Option	Description
-n	Do not send a warning message to the `syslog` facility when shutting down.

▶ **See Also** power.conf (142), pmconfig (145)

Power Management Configuration File (/etc/ power.conf)

`/etc/power.conf`

The `/etc/power.conf` file is the configuration file for the Solaris power management system. It is a plain text file and can be manually edited.

This file is read by the `pmconfig` utility and sets the properties for the power management daemon (`powerd`). The file contains only two types of entries: *device entries* and *system entries*.

Device Entry Format

`device threshold dependents`

Field	Required?	Description
`device`	Required	The name of the device to configure. Although full SCSI names can be used, it is usually easiest to use the relative path name such as `/dev/fb1` instead. If the relative path begins with `/devices`, the `/devices` part can be omitted.
`threshold`	Required	This field specifies the number of seconds of idle time that must pass before a specific component under power management shuts down. If a value of `-1` is used, power management for the specified device is disabled.
`dependents`	Optional	Optional devices that can be specified. Dependent devices must be idle and shut off before the power-managed device can be shut off. Usually these devices are not physically connected to a power-managed device (such as a keyboard).

System Entry Format

`keyword threshold time-of-day`

Field	Description
`keyword`	One of the special keywords given in the following table.
`threshold`	Idle time, in seconds, required.
`time-of-day`	Period of the day during which the action is allowed. Times are specified as a pair of *hh:mm* times. To have a time-of-day from 8:00 AM to 11:00 AM would be specified as follows: 8:00 11:00

Keyword	Description
shutdown	Shut down the system after the idle threshold has been exceeded. The current time must also be within the *time-of-day* time span.
noshutdown	Disable automatic shutdowns.
autowakeup	Shut down the system after the idle threshold has been exceeded and the current time is within the *time-of-day* time span. Restart the system when the current time is equal to the end time of the time span. Not all hardware has the capability to do this.
default	Allow the system to assume its default behavior. This behavior depends on the hardware. Consult the manuals that came with the hardware.
unconfigured	Disable automatic shutdowns. This keyword is only set before the system has been rebooted for the first time.

Other keywords are also supported by the power management system. The format of configuration lines using these keywords is given here.

Special Keyword	Description
ttychars *maxchar*	Specify a maximum number of tty characters that can be read before the system is considered non-idle. The default value of *maxchar* is 0.
loadaverage *maxload*	Specify a maximum load average that can be achieved before the system is considered non-idle. The default value of *maxload* is 0.04.
diskreads *maxdr*	Specify a maximum number of disk reads that can be performed before the system is considered non-idle. The default value of *maxdr* is 0.
nfsreqs *maxnfsrq*	Specify the maximum number of NFS requests that can be sent or received before the system is considered non-idle. The default value of *maxnfsrq* is 0. Null requests are not counted toward the total.
idlecheck *pathname*	Specify a pathname to a program that is run to check if the system is idle or not. The return code of the program should be the system idle time given in minutes. By default, the idlecheck parameter is not set.

U.S. EPA EnergyStar Compliance and Sun Desktops

Starting with Sun desktop systems manufactured after September 1995, the U.S. Environmental Protection Agency (EPA) mandated that all desktops be set (by default) to power down after a certain amount of idle time to conserve energy. Sun systems will shut down after 30 minutes of idle time, unless this option is changed during installation or by editing the /etc/power.conf file.

The following lines are in the /etc/power.conf on a freshly installed Solaris system.

```
/dev/kbd            1800
/dev/mouse          1800
/dev/fb             0 0        /dev/kbd /dev/mouse
autoshutdown        30         9:00 9:00              default
```

Configuring the Power Management System (pmconfig)

/usr./sbin/pmconfig [*options*]   pmconfig

The power management system is configured at boot time using the pmconfig command. There is no need to run this command manually; it is run automatically when the system starts up. It works by reading the /etc/power.conf to determine the proper configuration and then sends the appropriate commands to the Power Management daemon.

Option	Description
-r	Restore all power management configuration options to original settings.

▶ **See Also** powerd (142), /etc/power.conf (142)

PROM Level Booting

Boot Configuration Parameters (eeprom)

/usr/sbin/eeprom [*options*] [*param=value*]   eeprom

The eeprom command can be used to set or display boot configuration parameters stored in the NVRAM. eeprom will also detect and report any corrupted EEPROM settings. If no value is given, the current value of the parameter is displayed. If a value is specified, the parameter is set to the new value.

Option	Description
-	Read the parameters and values from standard input, one line at a time.
-f *device*	The EEPROM device is the device specified by device.

Boot Configuration Parameters

Parameter	Description	Default Value
auto-boot?	Automatically boot after a reset or when the power is turned on.	true
ansi-terminal?	Interpret ANSI escape sequences.	true
boot-command	Auto-boot command.	boot
boot-device	Define the default boot device.	disk net
boot-file	File to boot.	emtpy-string
boot-from	Where to boot from, including the device and file.	vmunix
boot-from-diag	Define the diagnostic boot device.	le() unix
diag-device	Define the diagnostic boot source.	net
diag-file	Define the diagnostic boot file.	empty-string
diag-level	Diagnostic level (off, min, and max, menus).	platform-dependent
diag-switch?	Specify if the system is to run in diagnostic mode.	true
fcode-debug	Include Fcodes plug-in parameters.	false
input-device	Default input device to use upon booting (keyboard, ttya, and ttyb).	keyboard
keyboard-click?	Enable keyboard clicks for key presses.	false
load-base	Define the client program load address.	16384

continues >>

ed

Parameter	Description	Default Value
local-mac-address?	Use network device drivers rather than the system MAC address.	false
mfg-mode	POST mode (off or chamber).	off
mfg-switch?	Continuously repeat system diagnostics until **STOP+A** is pressed.	false
nvramrc	NVRAMRC contents.	empty-string
oem-banner	Define the custom OEM banner (if oem-banner? is set to true).	emtpy-string
oem-banner?	Use custom OEM banner.	false
oem-logo	Define the custom OEM logo if oem-logo? is set to true. Must be a byte array in hexadecimal.	no-value
oem-logo?	Use custom OEM logo.	false
output-device	Output device to use upon boot (screen, ttya, or ttyb).	screen
sbus-probe-list	Probe order for the SBus slots.	0123
screen-#columns	Screen width (characters per line).	80
screen-#rows	Screen height.	34
scsi-initiator-id	Host adapter SCSI bus (0 through 7).	7
security-mode	Set the system security level (none, command, full). If the mode is set to full, a PROM password is required to logon.	
security-password	Define the firmware password if security-mode is set to full.	no-value
selftest-#megs	Define the amount of RAM to test at boot-time (in MB).	1
sunmon-compat	Use the Sun restricted monitor prompt.	false

continues >>

>>continued

Parameter	Description	Default Value
tpe-link-test?	Enable 10BaseT link test.	true
ttya-mode	Set the mode for TTYA by defining five fields: *baud rate*, *data bits*, *parity*, *stop bits*, and *handshake* (-,h,s). Example: 9600,8,n,1,s	9600,8, n,1,-
ttyb-mode	Set the mode for TTYB by defining five fields: *baud rate*, *data bits*, *parity*, *stop bits*, and *handshake* (-,h,s). Example: 9600,8,n,1,s	9600,8, n,1,-
ttya-ignore-cd	Ignore carrier detect.	true
ttyb-ignore-cd	Ignore carrier detect.	true
ttya-rts-dtr-off	Do not use DTR and RTS.	false
ttyb-rts-dtr-off	Do not use DTR and RTS.	false
use-nvramrc?	Run NVRAMRC commands on boot.	true
version2?	PROM starts in Version 2 mode if possible.	true
watchdog-reboot?	Reboot after watchdog reset.	false

Example	Description
eeprom input-device	Show the input device to use when the system boots.
eeprom input-device=ttya	Set the boot-time input device to TTYA.

Shutdowns and Rebooting

Restarting the Operating System (reboot)

reboot   /usr/sbin/reboot [*options*]

The reboot command is used to restart the system kernel in the normal multiuser run state. It is recommended that shutdown be used instead to warn users of the reboot. The reboot is logged by the syslog facility.

Option	Description
-d	Dump core before rebooting.
-l	Do not log the reboot to syslog.
-n	Do not sync the filesystems before the reboot. The failure to sync the filesystems can potentially corrupt data and is not recommended.
-q	Quick reboot. Processes are not shut down before the reboot.

Example	Description
reboot	Perform a normal orderly reboot.
reboot -ql	Perform a quick, unlogged reboot of the system.

Halting the Kernel (halt)

/usr/sbin/halt [*options*]   halt

The halt command is used to halt the system. Any information that is waiting to be written to the disks is written and the processor is stopped. The halt is logged using the syslog facility, unless the -n or -q option is used. If possible, use the shutdown command instead of halt because halt does not run the rc0 stop scripts as shutdown does.

Option	Description
-l	Do not log the username of the user who performed the halt.
-n	Do not sync the disks before halting.
-q	Quick halt. This option quickly halts the system without attempting an orderly shutdown process and writes out pending data.
-y	Allow halts from a dialup connection.

Example	Description
halt -l	Halt the system and do not log the username of the user executing the command.
halt -qy	Quick halt from a dial-up terminal.

Reboot or Shutdown (shutdown)

/usr/sbin/shutdown [*options*] [*message*]

The /usr/sbin/shutdown command is used to both reboot and shut down the system. Its function is to change the init state of the system.

Option	Description
-g *time*	Grace period. Wait the time specified by *time* (in seconds) before shutting down.
-i *state*	init state. For a complete listing of init/run states, see "Run States" (p. xxx).
-y	Automatically respond YES to confirm the shutdown when prompted. If this is excluded, the root user must confirm the shutdown after the command has been issued; otherwise the shutdown will be aborted.
message	An optional message can be specified that will be shown to all users logged into the system before shutting down.

There are two versions of shutdown available on Solaris systems:

System	Shutdown	Description
System V version	/usr/sbin/ shutdown	Slower than the UCB version because it takes time to run all the stop scripts in rc0.d/. This version will kill all processes before shutting down. This is the recommended version to use.
UCB version	/usr/ucb/ shutdown	Faster than the System V version. It does not run the scripts in rc0.d and only kills all non–single-user processes.

Example	Description
#/usr/sbin/shutdown ➥-i5 -g0 -y	Reboot immediately. No grace period. No confirmation required.
#/usr/sbin/shutdown ➥-iS -g0	Reboot to single-user mode. Must confirm shutdown when prompted.
#/usr/sbin/shutdown ➥-i5-g60 -y "SYSTEM ➥GOING DOWN FOR REPAIRS"	Shut down and remove power when done, if possible. Wait one minute (60 seconds) before doing so. Do not ask for confirmation. Display warning message.

Run States

Run State	Description
0	■ Stop system services, including servers and daemons.
	■ Terminate all running processes.
	■ Unmount all filesystems.
	■ Stop operating system.
	■ Safe to remove power.
1	■ Single-user state, only console is active.
	■ Stop system services, including servers and daemons.
	■ Terminate all running processes, although not all user processes may be terminated.
	■ Unmount all filesystems.
2	■ Set the TIMEZONE variable.
	■ Mount the /usr filesystem.
	■ Remove all files in /tmp and /var/tmp, as well as UUCP temp files.
	■ Initialize network interface.
	■ Start the cron daemon.
	■ Start sendmail and printer (lp) services.
	■ No NFS in this run state.
	■ Network as a client—server functions not started.
3	■ Set the TIMEZONE variable.
	■ Mount the /usr filesystem.
	■ Remove all files in /tmp and /var/tmp, as well as UUCP temp files.
	■ Initialize network interface.
	■ Start the cron daemon.
	■ Start sendmail and printer (lp) services.
	■ NFS services are started.

continues >>

>>continued

Run State	Description
4	■ Not used. (Available for your use.)
5	■ Stop system services, including servers and daemons.
	■ Terminate all running processes.
	■ Unmount all filesystems.
	■ Stop operating system.
	■ Remove power if possible (this feature depends on what hardware is used).
	■ Safe to remove power.
6	■ Reboot.
	■ Terminate all running processes.
	■ Unmount all filesystems.
	■ Reboot to initdefault entry in /etc/inittab.
S,s	■ Single-user state, only console is active.
	■ Terminate all user processes.
	■ Filesystems required for multiuser logins are not mounted.

inittab

innittab

Solaris uses a program called init to start up processes at boot time, usually servers and daemons. This program is controlled by a file called /etc/inittab. The file is a plain text file and can be manually edited.

Each line of the file consists of four fields:

identifier   run state   action   process

identifier

A two-character identifier that is unique to the process to be started. For example, the console control process (ttymon) can be identified by co. Both numbers and letters are allowed.

run state

Specifies the run states in which to spawn the process. The run state can be an integer between 0 and 6, or S (for single-user mode), corresponding to the Solaris run states (see "Run States," p. 151).

More than one state can be specified. For processes that should be started under normal, multiuser conditions, the run state should be set to 3. For a process that is to be started under all run states, leave this field blank.

If the run state is changed, as in the case of a reboot rather than a shutdown, all processes in the inittab that do not have the new run state listed will be sent a SIGTERM signal. The process is then allowed five seconds to terminate. If, after this time, the process has not terminated, a SIGKILL signal is sent.

action

The *action* field specifies how to handle the process to be started. The action can be one of 11 defined keywords.

Keyword	Description
respawn	Start the process if it is not already running. If the process dies it is restarted.
wait	Start the process and wait for it to finish. Commands with the wait action are only executed once per run state.
once	Start the process and do not wait for it to finish.
boot	Run the process only at boot-time. Do not wait and do not restart it if it dies.
bootwait	The process is run when the system switches from single to multiuser states. Once the process is started, it waits for its termination.
pwerfail	The process is started when init receives a SIGPWR signal (power failure).
powerwait	The process is started when init receives a SIGPWR signal (power failure). init will then wait for the process to finish.
off	If the process is running, it is killed. This is done by sending a SIGTERM, waiting five seconds, and then sending a SIGKILL.
ondemand	Same as respawn.
initdefault	This process is started when and only when the inittab is initially read. Note that if the run-state field is blank or 0123456, it will cause the system to continuously boot and become unusable.
sysinit	The process is started before the console is activated (displaying the login: prompt).

process

The *process* field represents the actual command to be run. This command can be any valid Solaris command line. The command line is actually passed to the Bourne Shell (sh) via an sh -c exec call. An example of an inittab file follows:

```
ap::sysinit:/sbin/autopush -f /etc/iu.ap
fs::sysinit:/sbin/rcS                        >/dev/console 2>&1
</dev/console
is:3:initdefault:
p3:s1234:powerfail:/usr/sbin/shutdown -y -i5 -g0 >/dev/console
2>&1
s0:0:wait:/sbin/rc0                          >/dev/console 2>&1
</dev/console
s1:1:wait:/usr/sbin/shutdown -y -iS -g0        >/dev/console
2>&1 </dev/console
s2:23:wait:/sbin/rc2                         >/dev/console 2>&1
</dev/console
s3:3:wait:/sbin/rc3                          >/dev/console 2>&1
</dev/console
s5:5:wait:/sbin/rc5                          >/dev/console 2>&1
</dev/console
s6:6:wait:/sbin/rc6                          >/dev/console 2>&1
</dev/console
fw:0:wait:/sbin/uadmin 2 0                    >/dev/console 2>&1
</dev/console
of:5:wait:/sbin/uadmin 2 6                    >/dev/console 2>&1
</dev/console
rb:6:wait:/sbin/uadmin 2 1                    >/dev/console 2>&1
</dev/console
sc:234:respawn:/usr/lib/saf/sac -t 300
co:234:respawn:/usr/lib/saf/ttymon -g -h -p "`uname -n`
console login: " -T sun -d /dev/console -l console -m
ldterm,ttcompat
```

Automatically Starting Services When Booting

Automatically Starting Services When Booting

Write the start/stop script using this basic format:

1. Copy the script to /etc/init.d/*servicename*.

2. Link the service start/stop script into the correct run state directory.

    ln /etc/init.d/*servicename* /etc/rcrunstate.d/SNN*servicename*

3. Link the service start/stop script into the correct run state directory. K scripts are used to kill processes and S scripts are used to start processes when entering the run state. Also note that K scripts are executed before the S scripts.

    ln /etc/init.d/*servicename* /etc/rcrunstate.d/KNN*servicename*

Field	Description
servicename	The name of the service or command to run (for example, webserver, snmp, and so on).
runstate	The run state that this service will be started in. This is usually 2 or 3. See "Run States" (p. 151).
NN	A unique number specifying the order in which to run multiple scripts. Use 99 if this is to be the last service started.

rc.local Replaced

Starting with Solaris 2, /etc/rc and /etc/rc.local are no longer used. They have been replaced with start/stop scripts in /etc/init.d.

Basic Format of Start/Stop Scripts

```
#!/bin/sh
#Solaris startup script
#

case "$1" in
start)
            #Commands to start service
            ;;
stop)
            #Commands to stop service
            ;;
esac
```

8

User Management

Basic User Management Tasks

Adding a User (useradd)

useradd

1. Create a new account for a user

   `useradd [options] username`

2. Set the password for the new user:

   `passwd username`

The `/usr/sbin/useradd` command is used to add new users to the system. The command edits the `/etc/passwd`, `/etc/shadow`, and `/etc/group` files to include the new user. It is possible to add a new user by manually editing these two files—however, it is not recommended. The `useradd` command should be used to add new accounts whenever possible. The `useradd` command does not set a password for the account. The `passwd` command should be run after adding the account. Also, by default, the new account is set to use the `/sbin/sh` shell. Most users prefer the `csh` or `ksh` shells. If the user shell is changed (using the `-s` option), be sure that any files in the `/etc/skel` directory are meant to use the new shell. The options given in the following section explain all of the different parameters that can be set when creating a new user.

Option	Description
-b *basedir*	Set the base directory of the system to *basedir*. Subsequent `useradd` commands will set the user's home directory to *basedir/login* if the `-d` option is not specified.
-c *comment*	Set the comment field to the string specified by *comment*. It is recommended to enclose the comment in quotes, but it is not necessary. The comment is usually the full name of the user or description of the account. This is the information that is shown by the `finger` command.
-D	Display the default values for `useradd`. By default these values are as follows: ■ `group = other,1` ■ `base_dir = /home` ■ `skel = /etc/skel` ■ `shell = /sbin/sh`

continues >>

Option	Description
	■ invalid = 0 (for use with the -f option) ■ expire = (not set) The -D option can also be used to set new default values, such as useradd -D -s/sbin/csh.
-d *homedir*	Set the home directory of the new user to the directory specified by *homedir*. If omitted, the default home directory is *basedir*/*login*, where *basedir* is the system base directory and *login* is the new user login name.
-e *expiration_date*	Expire the account (lock the account) on the specified date. The date can be specified in the following formats: ■ 2/7/99 ■ "February 7, 1999" Expiration dates are used to create temporary accounts for users.
-f *days*	Lock (invalidate) the account if it has not been used in the number of days, specified by *days*. Setting this option can increase the security of the system by locking inactive and possibly vulnerable accounts. However, if the number of days is set too low, it can be a nuisance.
-g *group*	Set the group membership of the new account. By default the group is set to other. Either the name (a string) or number (an integer) can be used to specify the group.
-G *other_group*	Set the supplementary group of a new account. Users can belong to more than one group, and this option sets the secondary group membership (*other_group*). Either the name (a string) or number (an integer) can be used to specify the group.
-k *skeldir*	Specify a skeleton directory. The skeleton directory contains files (such as .cshrc, .profile, and so on) that are copied to the new user's home directory. Any files that are in the skeleton directory are copied to all new accounts.
-m	Make the new directory. If the new user's home directory does not already exist, it is created and skeleton files (refer to -k *skeldir*, earlier in this table) are copied.

continues >>

>>continued

Option	Description
-o	Duplicate a user account, using the same UID number.
-s *shell*	Set the user shell to *shell*. The shell must be specified by a fully qualified path name (such as /sbin/csh). By default the shell is set to /sbin/sh.
-u *UID*	Set the user ID number to *UID*. By default a new UID is assigned that is one greater than the highest UID already assigned. New UIDs must be less than MAXUID as defined in /sys/param.h.

Third-Party Shells and the /etc/shells File

If a new user account is created and the user can log in via telnet, but cannot FTP to the system, check the /etc/shells file. All user shells must be listed in /etc/shells for FTP access to work. If a non-standard shell is set as a user's shell (such as **tcsh** or **zsh**), be sure to add the shell to /etc/shells.

Example	Description
useradd -c "John Smith" ➡smithj	Add a new user account for the user John Smith with the login name smithj.
useradd -c "Guest" -e ➡1/1/99 guest	Create a temporary guest account that expires on January 1, 1999.
useradd -c "John Smith" ➡-m -d/home2/smithj ➡smithj	Add a new user account for John Smith with a new home directory at /home2/smithj.

Modifying an Existing User Account (usermod)

usermod

1. Make sure that the user is not currently logged in:

   ```
   finger
   last username
   ```

2. Modify the user account:

   ```
   usermod username
   ```

After an account has been created using the useradd command, it can be modified using the usermod command. The usermod options are very similar to useradd and can modify any of the parameters set by the useradd command. As with useradd, the command changes the /etc/passwd and /etc/shadow files, which can also be done by manually editing the files. However, manual editing is not recommended.

Option	Description
-b *basedir*	Set the base directory of the system to *basedir*. Subsequent useradd commands will set the user's home directory to *basedir*/*login* if the -d option is not specified.
-c *comment*	Set the comment field to the string specified by comment. It is recommended to enclose the comment in quotes, but this is not necessary. The comment is usually the full name of the user or description of the account.
-d *homedir*	Set the home directory of the new user to the directory specified by *homedir*. If omitted, the default home directory is *basedir*/*login*, where *basedir* is the system base directory and *login* is the new user login name.
-e *expiration _date*	Expire the account (lock the account) on the specified date. The date can be specified in the following formats: ■ 2/7/99 ■ "February 7, 1999" Expiration dates are used to create temporary accounts for users.
-f *days*	Lock (invalidate) the account if it has not been used in the number of days specified by *days*. Setting this option can increase the security of the system by locking inactive and possibly vulnerable accounts. However, if the number of days is set too low, it can be a nuisance.
-g *group*	Set the group membership of the new account. By default, the group is set to other. Either the name (a string) or number (an integer) can be used to specify the group.
-G *other_group*	Set the supplementary group of a new account. Users can belong to more than one group, and this option sets the secondary group membership (*other_group*). Either the name (a string) or number (an integer) can be used to specify the group.
-l *login*	Change the login name to *login*.
-m	Move the home directory, creating the new directory if it does not exist. The home directory is created and skeleton files (see the preceding table's useradd options) are copied.

continues >>

>>continued

Option	Description
-s *shell*	Set the user shell to *shell*. The shell must be specified by a fully qualified path name (such as /sbin/csh). By default the shell is set to /sbin/sh.
-u *UID*	Set the user ID number to *UID*. By default a new UID is assigned that is one greater than the highest UID already assigned. New UIDs must be less than MAXUID as defined in /sys/param.h.

Modifying Active Accounts

When modifying a user account, the user cannot be logged in during the changes. If the user is logged in, usermod will return an error (error code 6).

Example	Description
usermod -l jsmith smithj	Change a user's login name from smithj to jsmith.
usermod -c "system op" ➟manager	Modify the comment field of the user account manager from "system admin" to "system op".
usermod -d/home2/smithj ➟-m smithj	Move a user's home directory from /home/smithj to /home2/smithj.

Deleting an Existing User Account (userdel)

userdel

1. Lock the user account (this step and step 2 are not necessary, but are recommended):

   passwd -l *username*

2. Wait until the next backup is performed.

3. Delete the user account:

   userdel [*options*] *username*

Accounts are deleted using the userdel command. This command removes the account entries from the /etc/passwd and /etc/shadow files. Optionally, userdel can also remove the user's home directory and all files contained in it. The /etc/passwd and /etc/shadow files can be manually edited to remove accounts in a similar manner—however, this is not recommended.

One alternative to immediately deleting unwanted accounts is to lock
the account for a while and then delete it. This will render the account
unusable—and yet, if for some reason something needs to be recovered from
the account, it will be available. It is recommended to lock the account until
the next backup is performed and only then delete the account.

Option	Description
-r	Remove the user's home directory when the account is deleted. The user's home directory and all contents will be permanently deleted, and will not be able to be recovered (unless a backup exists).

Remove Quotas Before Deleting the Account

Using `userdel` to delete a user does not remove a user's quota limits if set.
Before deleting a user, remove the user's quota limits using `edquota`. Then
update with `quotacheck`, and then use `userdel` to delete the account.
Although this is not necessary, it will keep excess information from building
up in `filesystem` quota files.

Example	Description
userdel smithj	Delete the user smithj but do not delete the home directory.
userdel -r smithj	Delete the user smithj and remove the associated home directory.

▶ **See Also** "Locking an Existing User Account" (163)

Ancillary User Management Tasks

Locking an Existing User Account (passwd -l)

passwd -l *username*   passwd -l

It may be necessary in some situations to temporarily disable a user
account. This can be done by setting the account entry in /etc/shadow
to show that the account is locked (*LK* in the password field). This is
done by using the **passwd** command. Note that when an account is
locked, the current password is lost. Therefore, a new password must be
set to unlock an account.

continues >>

>>*continued* If an account is suspected of being used for malicious purposes or some form of cracking, the account should be locked as soon as possible. The ability to lock accounts is also useful when an account is to be deleted. In this case, the account can be locked for a while until it is absolutely certain that nothing in the account is of any value, at which point it is deleted.

Example	Description
passwd -l smithj	Lock the account smithj.
passwd smithj	Unlock the account smithj, and reset the passwd.

▶ **See Also** "Deleting an Existing User Account" (162)

Changing an Existing User Password (passwd)

passwd   passwd *username*

Users commonly forget their passwords, in which cases the passwords must be changed. Also, after a new account is created using the useradd command, the passwd command must be used to set the password. This is done using the passwd command as root.

This is the same procedure that is used to unlock an account after it has been locked using the passwd -l command. Note that only the first six characters of the password are significant. The last two are basically ignored.

Prior to Solaris 2.5, the passwd command changed only the user's password in the file /etc/shadow on the local host. If NIS was running, the yppasswd command was used to change the user's password in the NIS database, and if NIS+ was running, the nispasswd command was used to change the password in the NIS+ database. However, in Solaris 2.5 and later, the passwd command, by default, changes the user's password in the first password source listed in the file /etc/nsswitch.conf. The commands yppasswd and nispasswd still exist for backward compatibility, but their use is discouraged. They are, in fact, just links to the passwd command.

For more information, please refer to Chapter 10, "Security," starting on page 207.

Example	Description
passwd smithj	Change the password for the account smithj.
passwd -r *files*	Change the password on the local host.
passwd -r nis	Change the password in the NIS database.
passwd -r nisplus	Change the password in the NIS+ database.

Switching Users and Changing to the Root User (su)

1. Use the su command to switch to a new user: su

   su [*options*] [*username*]

2. Enter password when prompted.

The su command is used to switch users, changing the effective user ID number of the user. By default, if no login name is specified, the su command attempts to change the user to the root user.

If the user invoking the su command is already root (uid=0), then the user is immediately switched to the other user. Otherwise, the user is prompted for the password of the other user account.

Users of the su command are logged to /var/adm/sulog.

Option	Description
-	If a dash (-) is given on the command line before the user-name, the other user's environment is used. This simulates logging in as the other user.

Example	Description
su	Switch to root.
su smithj	Switch to the user smithj.
su - smithj	Switch to the user smithj and use the environment variables (including path) of smithj.

Checking the Password File for Errors (pwck)

pwck

If the password file (/etc/passwd) is never manually edited, there is little chance that it will be corrupted when adding, deleting, or modifying users. Occasionally, however, slight problems may arise with the file. The pwck utility can be used to check the password file for common problems. Not all of the problems that pwck reports are serious, and each error reported should be taken on a case-by-case basis. For example, long usernames are not necessarily a problem, but should be avoided.

The password file has the following format:

username:x:*UID*:*GID*:*comment*:*home_directory*:*shell*

Parameter	Description
Number of fields	Each entry must have seven fields delimited by a :.
Login name	Login names must be eight or fewer characters.
User ID (*UID*)	All user IDs (UIDs) must be less than MAXUID as defined in sys/param.h.
Group ID (*GID*)	Group IDs must be valid as listed in /etc/group.
Home directory	The home directory must exist.
Shell	The shell must exist. This does not check if the shell is in /etc/shells.

Example

```
root: x:0:1:Super-User:/:/sbin/sh
daemon: x:1:1::/:
bin: x:2:2::/usr/bin:
sys: x:3:3::/:
adm: x:4:4:Admin:/var/adm:
lp: x:71:8:Line Printer Admin:/usr/spool/lp:
smtp: x:0:0:Mail Daemon User:/:
uucp: x:5:5:uucp Admin:/usr/lib/uucp:
nuucp: x:9:9:uucp
Admin:/var/spool/uucppublic:/usr/lib/uucp/uucico
listen: x:37:4:Network Admin:/usr/net/nls:
nobody: x:60001:60001:Nobody:/:
noaccess: x:60002:60002:No Access User:/:
mulligan: x:100:10:John
Mulligan:/home/ouser/mulligan:/bin/tcsh
```

Checking the Group File for Errors (grpchk)

The grpchk utility checks the group file (/etc/group) for errors. The group file has the following format:

groupname:blank:GID:members

Parameter	Description
Number of fields	Each entry must have four fields.
Group name	All group names must be valid.
GroupID (GID)	All group IDs must be valid.
Number of groups	No user can belong to more groups than is specified in NGROUPS_MAX as defined in sys/param.h.
Login names	All login names must appear in the password file (/etc/passwd).

Example

The following is an example listing of a group file (/etc/group).

```
root: :0:root
other: :1:
bin: :2:root,bin,daemon
sys: :3:root,bin,sys,adm
adm: :4:root,adm,daemon
uucp: :5:root,uucp
mail: :6:root
tty: :7:root,tty,adm
lp: :8:root,lp,adm
nuucp: :9:root,nuucp
staff: :10:
student: :30:
faculty: :40:
gcg: :500:
www: :600:
daemon: :12:root,daemon
sysadmin: :14:
nobody: :60001:
noaccess: :60002:
```

Quotas

Checking a Single User's Disk Quota (quota)

quota   quota -v *username*

The quota command can be used to check a user's ufs disk quota including disk usage and quota limits. Non-root users can use the quota command to check their own quotas and disk usage, but only the root user can specify a username on the command line to check other users. When used without any options, quota will only report any exceeded quotas.

Quotas are set using the edquota utility.

Option	Description
-v	Display all available information.

Output from quota -v is similar to the following:

```
Disk quotas for mulligan (uid 252):

Filesystem            usage quota  limit     timeleft  files
➥quota  limit     timeleft
/home/www/student   500 10000  10000                     0
➥0        0
```

The fields displayed are as follows:

Field	Description
Filesystem	The filesystem on which the quota is set.
Usage	The disk space used, in kilobytes.
Quota	The soft quota limit. If this limit is exceeded for longer than the time limit, the soft limit becomes the hard limit. Given in kilobytes.
Limit	The hard quota limit. At no point may this disk usage amount be exceeded. Given in kilobytes.
Timeleft	The time left before the soft limit becomes the hard limit.
Files	The number of files on the filesystem owned by the user.

Option	Description
Quota	The soft limit for the number of files allowed on the filesystem. If this limit is exceeded for longer than the time limit, the soft limit becomes the hard limit.
Limit	The hard limit for the number of files allowed on the filesystem. At no time may this number of files be exceeded.
Timeleft	The time left before the soft file limit becomes the hard limit.

Example	Description
quota	Check if the quota of the user invoking quota has been exceeded (non-root).
quota -v	Check the status of the quota if the user invoking quota has been exceeded (non-root).
quota smithj	Check if another user has exceeded his quota (root only).
quota -v smithj	Display all information about another user's quota (root only).

Reporting Filesystem Quotas (repquota)

/usr/sbin/repquota [*options*]   repquota

The repquota utility is used to report quota information for multiple users at a time. For displaying quota information for one user at a time, the quota command can be used. A filesystem, to be reported, must be specified unless the -a option is given, in which case all filesystems with quotas are reported.

Keeping Quotas Private

By default, Solaris allows all users of the system to use the repquota command. The repquota in /usr/sbin is actually a link to another file:

```
lrwxrwxrwx   1 root          22 Oct 21  1996
/usr/sbin/repquota -> ../lib/fs/ufs/repquota
```

continues >>

>>continued

The linked file is as follows:

```
-r-xr-xr-x    1 bin              8616 May  2  1996
../lib/fs/ufs/repquota
```

This file is executable by all. This means that all users on the system will be able to use the repquota utility.

In most cases this is not a problem, but if for some reason quota limits and disk usages are to be kept private, change the execute permission of /usr/lib/fs/repquota as follows (as root):

```
chmod 550 /usr/lib/fs/repquota
```

Option	Description
-a	Report all filesystems with quotas enabled. Filesystems with quotas enabled will have a rq in the mntopts field of /etc/vfstab.
-v	Report quota summaries for all users regardless of disk usage.

The output from repquota is similar to the following:

```
Block limits                              File limits
User      used   soft   hard  timeleft  used  soft  hard  timeleft
smithj -- 19   10000  10000              4     0     0
jonesb -  3121 10000  10000              77    0     0
smithk -    39 10000  10000              7     0     0
jonesw -  6393 10000  10000              175   0     0
smithr -  4271 10000  10000              135   0     0
```

Reporting Quotas over the Web

In some cases it may be desirable to allow users to check their quota usage over the Web. There are many ways to do this. The following CGI script is just one example of the way this can be done. It assumes that the username has been taken from an HTML form and passed to the $FORM_uname variable. It also assumes that $HOME is the base directory of the HTML files in the account, and that $WWW is the base of the URL (such as http://www.somedomain.com). It also uses two GIF images that are scaled using the WIDTH option in the <IMG> tags to display a bar graph representation of the quota usage. It should be noted that this script can be used by any user to check any other user's quota. If quotas are to be kept very private, this script should be modified.

```
if [ -z "$FORM_uname" ];then
FORM_uname="none"
fi

DATE=`date`
WWW=http://www.somedomain.com
QUOTA=`/usr/sbin/repquota -a¦ grep $FORM_uname ¦head -1¦ awk
➡'{print $4}'`

cat << EOM
<TITLE>Quota for $FORM_uname</TITLE>
<BODY BGCOLOR="#FFFFFF" TEXT="#000000">
<CENTER>
<TABLE BORDER=0 CELLPADDING=4 CELLSPACING=0 WIDTH=500>
<TR><TD BGCOLOR="#666699">
EOM

#check if there is no quota set for user
if [ -n "$QUOTA" ]; then
QUOTA=`/usr/sbin/repquota -a¦ grep $FORM_uname¦head -1 ¦ awk
➡'{print $5}'`
USED=`/usr/sbin/repquota -a¦ grep $FORM_uname ¦head -1 ¦ awk
➡'{print $3}'`
PUSED=`expr  $USED \* 100 / $QUOTA`
PFREE=`expr 100 - $PUSED`
NAME=`grep $FORM_uname /etc/passwd¦head -1¦awk '{FS=":";print
➡$5}'`

if [ $PFREE -lt 0 ];then
PFREE=1
fi

if [ -z "$NAME" ];then
NAME=`/usr/sbin/repquota -a¦ grep $FORM_uname¦head -1 ¦ awk
➡'{print $1}'`
fi
cat << EOM
<FONT FACE="Arial, Helvetica" SIZE=5 COLOR="#FFCC00">Quota for
$NAME</FONT>
<CENTER>
<TR><TD BGCOLOR="#FFFFCC">
EOM

if [ $PUSED -gt 100 ]; then
cat << EOM
<FONT FACE="Arial,Helvetica" COLOR="#FF0000" SIZE=4>
```

continues >>

>>continued

```
YOU ARE OVER YOUR QUOTA LIMIT</FONT>
<P>
<FONT FACE="Arial,Helvetica">Immediately remove unwanted files
➥from your account in order to decrease your disk usage.
➥</FONT><P>
EOM
fi

cat << EOM
<FONT FACE="Arial, Helvetica">You are currently using $USED KB
➥of disk space in your web account.  That means you are using
➥$PUSED% of your quota limit.<P><BR>
<FONT FACE="Arial Black, Arial, Helvetica"
➥SIZE=6><CENTER>$PUSED% FULL</FONT>
<BR CLEAR=both>
<IMG BORDER=0 WIDTH=$PUSED HEIGHT=20 HSPACE=0 ALT="$PUSED%
➥used"SRC="$WWW/images/blue_button.gif">
<IMG BORDER=0 WIDTH=$PFREE HEIGHT=20 HSPACE=0 ALT="$PFREE%
➥free"SRC="$WWW/images/blank_button.gif"><P><BR>
EOM
else
cat << EOM
<FONT FACE="Arial" COLOR="#FFCC00" SIZE=5>NO QUOTA</FONT>
<TR><TD BGCOLOR="#FFFFCC">
<FONT FACE="Arial, Helvetica">
No quota set for $FORM_uname. Perhaps you typed the user name
➥incorrectly.
Please resubmit your query.
<BR CLEAR=both><P><BR>
<A HREF="$WWW/quota.html">Try again.</A>
EOM
fi
echo "</TABLE><PRE></CENTER>"
echo "$DATE: $REMOTE_HOST checked $FORM_uname" >>
➥$HOME/log/quota.log
```

The accompanying HTML form is given below:

```
<FORM METHOD=GET ACTION="/cgi-bin/quotacheck">
<FONT FACE="Arial, Helvetica">
Enter your username: </FONT>
<INPUT NAME="uname" SIZE=15><P>
<CENTER>
<FONT FACE="Arial, Helvetica" SIZE=3>
<INPUT TYPE=RESET VALUE="Reset form">
<INPUT TYPE=SUBMIT VALUE="Press to Check"></FONT>
</FORM>
```

Editing User Quotas (edquota)

edquota *username*

The edquota command is used to edit quotas of individual users. By default, edquota invokes the vi editor to edit the quota limits, but this can be changed by setting the EDITOR environment variable to the desired editor. Only the root user may edit quotas.

When invoked, the edquota utility will create a temporary file that can be edited to set the quota. The quota will only be updated after the editor exits. The temporary file will have the following form:

```
fs mountpoint blocks (soft = slimit, hard =hlimit) inodes
➥(soft =slimit, hard = hlimit)
```

mountpoint is the mount point for the filesystem. The blocks section sets the soft and hard limits for the disk usage (given in 1,024 byte blocks). The inodes section sets the soft and hard limits for the number of files allowed on the filesystem that are owned by the user. Hard limits cannot be exceeded under any circumstances. Soft limits can be exceeded for a specified time limit before the soft limit becomes a hard limit.

Option	Description
-p	Use prototype user. Copy the quota of the specified user and apply the quota to the user whose quota is being edited.
-t	Change the soft limit time for the filesystem. If set to 0, the default time is used as defined in /usr/include/sys/fs/ufs_quota.h.

Setting New Quotas

If quotas are being set for the first time for a user, the quotacheck utility must be run for the quotas to take effect.

Example	Description
edquota smithj	Edit the quota for the user smithj.

Enabling/Disabling Quotas on a Filesystem (quotaon)

quotaon [*options*]

Before quotas can be used on `ufs` filesystems, the quota system must be enabled. This is done by using the `quotaon` command. Similarly, to disable quotas on a filesystem, the `quotaoff` command is used. Although quotas are turned on for filesystems as a whole, each user's quota limits are individually set.

The `quotaon` and `quotaoff` commands modify the `/etc/mnttab` file. When quotas are enabled, the filesytem entry will be marked `quota` under the `mntopts`. If the quotas are disabled using `quotaoff`, the entry will be marked `quotaoff`. This can be done manually, without using `quotaon` and `quotaoff`, but it is not recommended.

At boot time, quotas are enabled on any filesystems with `"rq"` in the `mntopts` field of `/etc/vfstab`.

Option	Description
-a (quotaon)	Enable all quotas on any filesystems with `"rq"` in the `mntopts` field of `/etc/vfstab`.
-v (quotaon)	Verbose. Report status after each filesystem quota is enabled.
-a (quotaoff)	Shut off quotas for all filesystems in `/etc/mnttab`.
-v (quotaoff)	Verbose. Report status after each filesystem quota is disabled.

Example	Description
quotaon -a	Turn on all quotas.
quotaoff -a	Turn off all quotas.
quotaon -av	Turn on all quotas, reporting which ones were enabled.

Updating Quotas (quotacheck)

quotacheck   `quotacheck [options]`

The `quotacheck` utility performs the following tasks on the specified filesystem (or all filesystems, if -a is used):

1. Examine each mounted ufs file system.

2. Build a table of current disk usage.

3. Compare disk usage against established quota limits.

4. Update the quota file, fixing any discrepancies.

It is necessary to run quotacheck after a quota has been set (using edquota) for each new user. It is also a good idea to run quotacheck once in a while to keep the quota files up to date and free from problems.

Safely Updating Quotas

Filesystems should not be very active while quotacheck is being run. Although it is not necessary to reboot into single-user mode, the less activity there is, the less chance there is for problems.

It is recommended that, as root, the wall command is used to urge users to save their work and log out before quotacheck is run.

Option	Description
-a	All filesystems. All filesystems that have rq in mntopts in the /etc/vfstab file, have a quota file, and are listed as ufs filesystems in /etc/mnttab are checked and updated.
-p	Update quota files in parallel.
-v	Verbose. Show quota information for all users. If omitted, quotacheck will report user information only if a change was made.

Example	Description
quotacheck -ap	Check all filesystems in parallel.
quotacheck /home	Check the /home filesystem.
quotacheck -v /home/⮕student	Check the /home/student filesystem, showing disk usage for all users.

9
Filesystems

Contents

Filesystem Overview and Description

Solaris Filesystem Layout

Under Solaris, hard disk storage is divided into *filesystems* (also known as *partitions*). Dividing the hard drive into sections allows common files to be grouped together. This makes sharing files over networks easier and generally improves the ability to manage the system.

The default Solaris installation is divided into three filesystems: /, /usr, and /export.

Solaris Filesystems

Filesystem	Description
/	The root filesystem. Usually files on the root filesystem are not shared across the network and are kept only on the local machine. System configuration files, such as those kept in /etc, are on the root filesystem. The root filesystem should be kept as small as possible if there is a separate /var filesystem. If it is simply a directory under the root filesystem, then / should be large because it will hold all the variable system logs and other variable size files.
/usr	The /usr fileystem. The /usr (pronounced "user") filesystem is usually much larger than the root filesystem and contains files that are to be shared across the network using NFS. Traditionally, the /usr filesystem was used to serve files that can be used on many computer architectures.
/export	If a Solaris system has a large amount of disk space available and is on a network, it can be used to share entire filesystems (such as root or swap space) with other diskless clients.

The Root Filesystem

Directory	Description
/dev	Device files for kernel and hardware
/dev/dsk	Disk devices

continues >>

Directory	Description
/dev/pts	Pseudo-terminal devices
/dev/rsdk	Raw disk devices (such as floppy drives)
/dev/rmt	Tape devices (such as tape backups)
/dev/sad	STREAMS administrative devices
/dev/term	Terminal devices
/etc	Configuration files that are unique to each host
/etc/acct	Accounting system configuration files
/etc/cron.d	cron configuration
/etc/default	Default configuration files for certain programs
/etc/dfs	Shared filesystem configuration
/etc/fs	Files used before /usr is mounted
/etc/inet	Internet configuration files
/etc/init.d	Scripts for startup and shutdown, as well as change of run state
/etc/lib	Shared libraries
/etc/lp	Printer service configuration files
/etc/mail	Mail service configuration files
/etc/net	Network service configuration files
/etc/opt	Optional software package configurations
/etc/rc0.d	Startup and shutdown scripts for run state 0
/etc/rc1.d	Startup and shutdown scripts for run state 1
/etc/rc2.d	Startup and shutdown scripts for run state 2
/etc/rc3.d	Startup and shutdown scripts for run state 3
/etc/saf	Files for the Service Access Facility
/etc/skel	Files for new accounts created using the useradd utility
/etc/sm	Status monitor information
/etc/sm.bak	Status monitor information backup
/etc/tm	Trademark information shown at boot time
/etc/uucp	UUCP configuration files

continues >>

>>continued

Directory	Description
/home	User files and home directories
/kernel	Platform-independent kernel modules
/mnt	Temporary mount point for mounting filesystems
/opt	Optional/third-party software packages and applications
/platform	Platform-dependent objects
/platform/ */kernel	Platform-dependent objects related to the UNIX kernel
/platform/ */lib	Platform-dependent objects related to shared libraries
/platform/ */sbin	Platform-dependent objects related to system binaries
/proc	Process information and tools
/sbin	System binaries required to boot before /usr is mounted
/tmp	Temporary files (all files are removed at boot time)
/var	Varying files that are host specific, yet are of an undetermined size, such as log files (/var/log/syslog or /var/adm/log)
/var/adm	Varying administrative files
/var/cron	cron log files
/var/mail	User mail files
/var/news	Files shown to users using the news command (not related to USENET)
/var/nis	NIS+ databases
/var/opt	Varying files created by optional software packages or applications
/var/preserve	vi and ex backup files
/var/sadm	Software management databases
/var/saf	Logging and accounting files for the Service Access Facility
/var/spool	Files used by mail services, printer services, and cron
/var/spool/lp	Printer spool files
/var/spool/ mqueue	Mail queue files (mail waiting to be sent)

continues >>

Directory	Description
/var/spool/pkg	Temporary space for packages being installed using the pkgadd utility
/var/spool/uucp	Queued UUCP processes
/var/spool/uucppublic	Files created by UUCP jobs
/var/tmp	Temporary files (not cleared at boot time)
/var/uucp	UUCP log files
/var/yp	Compatibility files for NIS and YP services
/var/spool/cron	Temporary files for cron and at
/var/spool/locks	Lock files

The usr Filesystem

Directory	Description
/usr/4lib	Binary Compatibility Package (BCP) libraries
/usr/bin	System utilities and binaries
/usr/bin/sunview1	Binary Compatibility Package (BCP) SunView executables
/usr/ccs	C Compiler System (CCS) files
/usr/ccs/bin	C compiler binaries
/usr/ccs/lib	Libraries for the C compiler
/usr/demo	Demonstration programs
/usr/dt	Common Desktop Environment (CDE) files
/usr/dt/bin	CDE binaries
/usr/dt/include	CDE include and header files
/usr/dt/lib	CDE libraries
/usr/dt/man	Online manual pages (man pages) for CDE
/usr/games	Game files

continues >>

>>continued

Directory	Description
/usr/include	Header files for use with C compilers
/usr/kernel	Platform-independent kernel modules
/usr/platform/	Platform-dependent objects
usr/lib	Program-specific libraries and programs that are not directly executed by users (such as sendmail)
/usr/lib/acct	Accounting binaries
/usr/lib/dict	Dictionary files and spelling databases
/usr/lib/ class	priocntrl and dispadmin files
/usr/lib/font	Description files for use with troff
/usr/lib/fs	Filesystem modules and programs that are not directly executed by users
/usr/lib/ iconv	iconv conversion tables
/usr/lib/libp	Profiled libraries
/usr/lib/ locale	Databases for localization of the system (languages, time zones, and so on)
/usr/lib/lp	Printer service databases and binaries that are not directly executed by users
/usr/lib/mail	Mail service programs (including sendmail)
/usr/lib/ netsvc	Internet files
/usr/lib/nfs	Network File System (NFS) files
/usr/lib/pics	Position Independent Code (PIC) files
/usr/lib/refer	Programs used by refer
/usr/lib/sa	System Activity Report (SAR) files
/usr/lib/saf	Service Access Facility (SAF) files
/usr/lib/spell	Binary Compatibility Package spelling files
/usr/lib/uucp	UUCP daemons
/usr/local	Local programs and utilities
/usr/net/ servers	Entry points for the Listen daemon

continues >>

Directory	Description
/usr/oasys	Framed Access Command Environment (FACE) package files
/usr/old	Old programs
/usr/openwin	OpenWindows software
/usr/sadm	System administration files
/usr/sadm/bin	Form and Menu Language Interpreter (FMLI) files
/usr/sadm/ install	Package management files
/usr/sbin	System administration binaries
/usr/sbin/ static	Statically linked programs to recover from problems
/usr/share	Platform-independent shared files
/usr/share/ man	Online manual pages
/usr/share/ lib	Platform-independent libraries and databases
/usr/share/ lib/keytables	Keyboard configuration files
/usr/share/ lib/mailx	mailx help files
/usr/share/ lib/nterm	Terminal tables for nroff
/usr/share/ lib/pub	Character sets
/usr/share/ lib/spell	spell databases and files
/usr/share/ lib/tabset	Tab-setting files
/usr/share/ lib/terminfo	Terminal information files for use with terminfo
/usr/share/ lib/tmac	nroff and troff macro files
/usr/share/ lib/zoneinfo	Time zone information

continues >>

>>continued

Directory	Description
/usr/share/src	Shared source code
/usr/snadm	SNAG files
/usr/ucb	University of California Berkeley (UCB) distribution files for compatibility
/usr/ucbinclude	University of California Berkeley (UCB) distribution header files
/usr/ucblib	University of California Berkeley (UCB) distribution library
/usr/vmsys	Framed Access Command Environment (FACE) files

The **export** Filesystem

Directory	Description
/export	The exported filesystem
/export/exec/platform	The /usr filesystem that is ready for export for the platform/architecture specified by platform
/export/exec/share	The /usr/share directory for export to all systems
/export/root/hostname	The root filesystem to be exported to the host specified by hostname
/export/root/swap/hostname	The swap file to be exported for the host specified by hostname
/.export/var/hostname	The /var filesystem to be exported to the host specified by hostname

Solaris Filesystem Description File (vfstab)

vfstab   /etc/vfstab

All of the Solaris filesystems are described in the vfstab file (/etc/vfstab). Each line in the vfstab file consists of seven space-delimited columns. The columns are as follows:

```
device to mount  device to fsck  mount point  FS type
➥fsck pass  mount at boot  mount options
```

Field	Description
device to mount	The name of the resource to mount. If a swap file is to be specified, the device to mount is the swap filename.
device to fsck	The raw device on which to perform a filesystem consistency check (fsck).
mount point	The default mount point.
FS type	The filesystem type (such as ufs, pcfs, nfs, or hsfs). If the resource is a swap file, the FS type is swap.
fsck pass	A number to determine when and in what order fsck will automatically check the filesystem.
mount at boot	Determine whether the filesystem should be mounted by mountall at boot time. If a swap file is being specified, mount at boot should be set to no.
mount options	Any mount options to be used when mounting the resource. See mount.

If a field does not apply or needs to be left blank, put a - in the column.

Constructing and Mounting New Filesystems

Constructing a New Filesystem (newfs)

newfs [*options*] *raw-device*   newfs

In previous versions of SunOS, new filesystems were created using the mkfs command. The newfs command has been added to ease the creation of UFS filesystems, acting as a front-end to the mkfs utility. The newfs command automatically determines all the necessary parameters to pass to mkfs to construct the new filesystem.

This command can only be used by the root user to create new filesystems, unless the new filesystem is on a removable floppy disk. If the new filesystem is on a disk, anyone can use newfs. The following options can be used with the newfs utility.

Option	Description
-a *abpc*	Alternate blocks per cylinder. This option applies only to SCSI devices reserved for bad block placement. The default value is 0.
-b *blocksize*	Block size. Specify the logical block size of the filesystem in bytes. Must be either 4096 or 8192. The default value is 8192.
-c *cpg*	Cylinders per cylinder group. This value must be in the range of 1 to 32. The default value is 16.
-C *max*	The maximum number of blocks that can be allocated together before a rotational delay is inserted. The default value depends on the filesystem: ■ 4K FS = 14 ■ 8K FS = 7 This option can be changed later using tunefs.
-d *delay*	Rotational delay. Specify the rotational spacing between blocks in a file and give it in milliseconds. This value can be changed later using the tunefs command. The default value depends on the type of drive.
-f *size*	Fragment size. The smallest number of bytes to allocate to a file. The value must be 2^n, where n can be in the range from 512 to the logical block size.
-i *bpi*	Bytes per inode. The number determines the total number of inodes in the filesystem. To allow for fewer inodes, use a large number. For more inodes, use a small number. The default value is 2048.
-m *freepct*	Minimum free space. Specify the amount of free space (expressed as a percentage of the total) to be maintained on the disk. Only the root user can write to the disk to exceed the minimum free space allowance. The default value is 10%.
-N	Display all parameters that would be used in creating the new filesystem, but do not actually create the filesystem or alter the disk in any way.
-n *rotpos*	Rotational positions. Specify the number of divisions in a cylinder group. The default value is 8.

continues >>

Option	Description
-o *optimize*	Optimization. Can be one of two options: ■ `space`: Minimize time spent allocating blocks. ■ `time`: Minimize space fragmentation on the disk. If the minimum free space (as given by -m) is less than 10%, space optimization is used.
-r *rpm*	Disk speed. Specify the speed of the disk in revolutions per minute. The default value is `3600`.
-s *sectors*	Disk sectors. Specify the size of the file system in sectors. The default is to use the entire filesystem.
-t *tpc*	Tracks per cylinder. Specify the number of tracks per cylinder on the disk. The default value depends on the drive.
-v	Verbose. All actions and informative messages are displayed.

Example	Description
newfs -v /dev/rdsk/ ➡c0t0d0s6	Create a new filesystem using all default values, showing all actions.
newfs -Nv /dev/rdsk/ ➡c0t0d0s8	Display information about a raw device but do not create a filesystem.

Constructing a New Filesystem (mkfs)

/usr/sbin/mkfs [*options*] *filesystem*   mkfs

The `mkfs` utility constructs new filesystems. All types of filesystems can be created using `mkfs`. Options that are common to all types of filesystems are specified, as usual, on the command line. Filesystem specific options are specified using the -o option.

Using the Front-End

The `newfs` utility has been added to Solaris to make the creation of new filesystems easier. It acts as a front-end for the `mkfs` utility. It is highly recommended that the `newfs` front-end be used to create new filesystems whenever possible. See "Constructing a New Filesystem (newfs).'"

Options for All Filesystems

Option	Description
-F	Filesystem type. This option can be used to specify the filesystem type. If this option is omitted, the /etc/vfstab and /etc/default/fs files are checked to determine a filesystem type.
-m	Show the command line that was used to create the specified filesystem. No changes are made to the filesystem.
-o	Use filesystem-specific options. (See subsequent tables.)
-V	Verbose. Show the command line but do not execute anything.

Options for New UFS Filesystems

The options used to create a new UFS filesystem are specified by keywords set to a specified value. In each case n is an integer.

Option	Description
apc=n	Reserved space for bad block replacement on SCSI devices. The default value is 0.
bsize=n	Logical block size of either 4096 (4K) or 8192 (8K). The default is 8192.
cgsize=n	Number of cylinders per cylinder group. The default value is 16.
fragsize=n	The smallest amount of space allocated to a file. The value must be 2^b where b is a number from 512 to the local block size. The default value is 1024.
free=n	The minimum amount of free space to maintain on the filesystem. The default value is 60.
gap=n	Rotational delay, given in milliseconds. The default value depends on the drive type.
maxcontig=n	The maximum number of blocks that can be allocated together before a rotational delay is inserted. The default value depends on the filesystem: ■ 4K systems: 14 ■ 8K systems: 7 This parameter can be changed later using tunefs.

continues >>

Option	Description
N	Do not construct the filesystem. Only show the parameters that would be used.
nbpi=n	Number of blocks per inode. The default value is 2048.
nrpos=n	Rotational positions for each cylinder. The default value is 8.
nsect=n	Number of sectors per track. The default value is 32.
ntrack=n	Number of tracks per cylinder. The default value is 16.
opt=type	Optimization type. The type can be one of the following: ■ s: Optimize for disk space. ■ t: Optimize for speed (time).
rps=n	Disk speed given in revolutions per second. The default value is 60.

Mounting and Unmounting Filesystems (mount, mountall)

```
/usr/sbin/mount [options] filesystem mountpoint
/usr/sbin/umount [options] mountpoint
```

mount, mountall

The mount and umount commands are used to mount and unmount filesystems. Mounting a filesystem attaches it to the existing filesystem hierarchy so that it can be used. A table of mounted filesystems is kept in the mnttab (pronounced mount-tab) file at /etc/mnttab.

Options for All Filesystem Types

Option	Description
-a	Mount all filesystems specified in /etc/vfstab as "mount at boot" in parallel if possible. If the umount command is being used, all filesystems listed in /etc/mnttab are unmounted.
-a mountpoints	If the umount command is being used, only the mount points listed are unmounted.
-F type	Specify the type of filesystem to mount.
-m	Mount filesystem without adding an entry to /etc/mnttab.
-o	Specify filesystem-specific mount options. Options should be separated by commas.

continues >>

>>continued

Option	Description
-O	Overlay. The filesystem is mounted over a currently mounted mount point. The underlying filesystem will not be usable after this operation.
-p	Print the filesystems in /etc/vfstab. No other options can be used with this option.
-r	Mount the filesystem as read-only.
-v	Print the filesystems in /etc/vfstab showing all information (verbose). No other options can be used with this option.
-V	Print the command line, but do not execute anything.

Options for Mounting UFS Filesystems

Option	Description
f	Fake entry. Add an entry to /etc/mnttab, but do not actually mount the filesystem.
intr	Allow keyboard interrupts to kill processes waiting for locked filesystems.
m	Mount the filesystem but do not add an entry to /etc/mnttab.
nointr	Do not allow keyboard interrupts to kill processes waiting for locked filesystems.
nosuid	Disallow suid execution of programs.
onerror= action	Specify the action to take on errors. The action can be one of four options: ■ panic: Force a system shutdown. ■ lock: Lock the filesystem. ■ umount: Force the filesystem to be unmounted. ■ repair: Perform an automatic fsck. The default option is panic.
quota	Enable quotas for the specified filesystem.
remount	Remount a currently mounted filesystem. To be used to change filesystems from read-only to read-write.

continues >>

Option	Description
ro	Mount filesystem as read-only.
rq	Mount filesystem as read and write with quotas enabled.
rw	Mount filesystem as read-write enabled.
toosoon=*time*	Specify the minimum time between filesystem inconsistencies that will signal a forced shutdown or repair. The time is specified in seconds (s), minutes (m), hours (h), days , weeks (w), or years (y), using the units shown. For example: 15h is 15 hours.

Checking and Tuning Filesystems

Checking and Fixing Filesystems (fsck)

The fsck utility is an interactive tool used to perform consistency checks   fsck
and repair filesystems. By default, the user will be asked for confirmation
before any corrective action takes place. Only the root user can fix disk
problems using fsck.

Possible Loss of Data

The fsck utility can fix many common disk problems. It should be noted,
however, that corrective actions can lead to loss of data on the filesystem.
The amount of data lost depends on the severity of the problem, and will be
reported at the end of the fsck execution.

To prevent potential problems, unmount filesystems before performing a
fsck whenever possible. If this is not possible, reboot immediately after
running fsck.

Options for All Filesystems

Option	Description
-F *type*	Specify filesystem type.
-m	Perform a sanity check on the filesystem but no repairs are made. This option can be used as a quick check to see if a filesystem is ready to be mounted.

continues >>

>>continued

Option	Description
-N	Answer no to all corrective-action questions.
-o	Use filesystem-specific options. Options must be given in a comma-delimited list.
-V	Print command lines but do not perform any actions.
-Y	Answer yes to all corrective action questions.

Options for UFS Filesystems

Option	Description
b=n	Treat block n as the filesystem super block. Super blocks can be found using the newfs utility with the -Vn option.
c	Convert table formats. Old format static tables are converted to new dynamic tables, and vice versa.
f	Force filesystem checks.
p	Preen. Check and fix filesystem without user interaction.
w	Perform fsck on writeable filesystems only.

Exit Code	Description
0	No errors or filesystem problems.
1	Incorrect fsck usage.
32	Filesystem is unmounted and needs to be checked.
33	Filesystem is mounted.
34	Can't check device.
36	Filesystem errors were found that cannot be corrected.
37	Signal encountered during execution.
39	Filesystem errors were found that cannot be corrected—abnormal termination.
40	No errors or filesystem problems.

Printing Filesystem Statistics and Filenames (ff)

ff   The ff utility can be used to print pathnames and inode numbers for all the files on a given filesystem. This command is similar to the ncheck utility.

Options for All Filesystems

Option	Description
-a *n*	Print files only if they have been accessed in *n* days.
-c *n*	Print files only if their status has changed in the last *n* days.
-F *type*	Specify the filesystem type.
-I	Print the inode numbers with associated pathnames.
-i *list*	Print only files with inodes given in *list*. The list must be a comma-delimited list of inumbers.
-l	Generate another list for file with multiple links.
-m *n*	Print files only if they have been written to or created in the last *n* days.
-n *filename*	Print files only if they have been modified in the last *n* days.
-o	Specify filesystem-specific options.
-p *prefix*	Prepend the prefix to each pathname listed.
-s	Show file sizes in bytes.
-u	Show file ownership.
-V	Print the command line, but do not perform any actions.

Options for UFS Filesystems Only

Option	Description
a	Print . and .. as well as other files.
m	Show file modes.
s	Print only setuid and special files.

Checking Free Disk Space (df)

The df command can be used to check free disk space on a filesystem.   df
Exported and remounted filesystems (such as /export or, sometimes,
/home) can occasionally be listed twice.

Option	Description
-a	Show disk space for all filesystems.
-b	Show only free disk space, in kilobytes.

continues >>

>>continued

Option	Description
-e	Show only the number of files free on the filesystem.
-F type	Specify the filesystem type. Used only with unmounted filesystems.
-g	Show all information (entire statvfs structure) for mounted filesystems.
-k	Display all information with allocations and free space given in kilobytes.
-l	Show local filesystems only. NFS filesystems are not shown.
-n	Print the filesystem type only.
-o options	Specify filesystem-specific options given as a comma-delimited list.
-P	Show all information given in 512-byte units.
-t	Show totals for disk statistics.
-v	Print the command line, but do not execute any actions.

Example Output of df

```
/                    (/dev/dsk/c0t0d0s0 ):  655122 blocks
➡461301 files
/proc                (/proc            ):       0 blocks
➡1959 files
/dev/fd              (fd               ):       0 blocks
➡0 files
/opt                 (/dev/dsk/c0t1d0s0 ):  351948 blocks
➡366443 files
/export              (/dev/dsk/c1t0d0s6 ): 6318772 blocks
➡502588 files
/stuff               (/dev/dsk/c0t1d0s6 ): 5439788 blocks
➡397744 files
/spare1              (/dev/dsk/c0t0d0s7 ): 1984568 blocks
➡499453 files
/spare2              (/dev/dsk/c0t2d0s5 ): 7803320 blocks
➡470011 files
/music               (/dev/dsk/c0t2d0s6 ): 2957202 blocks
➡469375 files
/tmp                 (swap             ):  866776 blocks
➡16166 files
/oldroot             (/dev/dsk/c0t2d0s0 ):  522688 blocks
➡340701 files
/home/marym          (/export/home/marym): 6318772 blocks
➡502588 files
```

Example Output of df -k

```
Filesystem              kbytes     used    avail capacity Mounted
➥on
/dev/dsk/c0t3d0s0       100935    27083    63762   30%    /
/dev/dsk/c0t2d0s6       384243   255164    90659   74%    /usr
/proc                        0        0        0    0%    /proc
fd                           0        0        0    0%    /dev/fd
/dev/dsk/c0t3d0s3       167631   129800    21071   87%    /var
/dev/dsk/c0t2d0s5        96048    11225    75223   13%    /tmp
/dev/dsk/c0t2d0s7       131718     1334   117214    2%
➥/var/tmp
/dev/dsk/c1t2d0s1     3939430  1348153  2197337   39%
➥/var/spool/news
/dev/dsk/c1t1d0s6       306418   142389   133389   52%    /home
/dev/dsk/c1t1d0s7       306418   261545    14233   95%
➥/home/staff
/dev/dsk/c0t0d0s6       306418   198473    77305   72%
➥/home/student
/dev/dsk/c0t0d0s7       306418   117572   158206   43%
➥/home/math
host2:/usr/local       631824   463824   104816   82%
➥/usr/local
host2:/opt             192416   154176    19000   90%    /opt
host2:/usr/share/man   631824   463824   104816   82%
➥/usr/share/man
host2:/usr/X11R6.1     631824   463824   104816   82%
➥/usr/X11R6.1
```

Labeling Filesystems (labelit)

The labelit utility is used to label filesystems and to print labels for   labelit
current filesystems. The filesystem must be unmounted before it can be
labeled. Disk labels are used by programs such as volcopy.

Option	Description
-F type	Specify the filesystem type.
-V	Print command line, but do not perform any actions.

List Pathnames and inumbers (ncheck)

The ncheck utility generates a list of pathnames with the associated   ncheck
inumbers for a block special device. A block special device can be specified
on the command line; otherwise, ncheck is run on all devices marked as
special in /etc/vfstab. Some options can be used for all filesystem types,
whereas other options are filesystem specific.

Options for All Filesystem Types

Option	Description
-a	Show . and .. when listing filenames.
-F	Specify the filesystem type on which to perform an ncheck.
-i *list*	Show only those files associated with the list of inumbers given. The list must be comma-delimited.
-o	Specifies filesystem-specific options. Given in a comma-delimited list.
-s	Show only setuid and special files. This option can be used to check the security of the system.
-V	Print the command line, but do not perform any actions.

Options for Use with UFS Filesystems

Option	Description
m	Print mode information for files.

Tuning a Filesystem (tunefs)

tunefs

After a filesystem has been unmounted, tunefs can be used to tune the performance and parameters of the disk. The filesystem must be in /etc/vfstab to be tuned.

Option	Description
-a *max*	Set the maximum number of blocks that will be written continuously before a rotational delay is inserted.
-d *delay*	Set the size of the rotational delay (in milliseconds) to insert between blocks.
-e *bpg*	Set the maxmium number of blocks per cylinder group.
-m *free*	Set the minimum amount of free space to maintain on the filesystem.
-o *type*	Set the type of filesystem optimization: ■ space: Optimize for space. ■ time: Optimize for speed (access time reduction).

Example	Description
tunefs -o time /home	Optimize the /home filesystem for speed.

Backups

Backing Up a Filesystem (ufsdump)

The ufsdump utility is used to back up filesystems. Either specific files or   ufsdump
entire filesystems can be dumped to the backup device (such as a tape
backup). By default, the backup is dumped to /dev/rmt/0.

Devices Must Be Inactive When Backing Up

It is very important that the filesystem being backed up is not active (being
read or written to). It should be either unmounted or in single-user mode
when ufsdump is running. Attempting to back up an active filesystem will
lead to data corruption and it may be impossible to restore files from the
backup.

Option	Description
a	Archive file. Create an archive table of contents to be used by ufsrestore to check if a file has been backed up.
b factor	Blocking factor. Specify the blocking factor to be used for tape devices. The default value is 20 blocks per write for tapes of 6,250 bytes/inch or less. Blocks are 512-byte blocks.
c	Use default values for cartridge backups rather than half-inch reel.
D	Dump to disk.
d bpi	Tape density. Set the tape density to bpi, or bytes per inch.
dumplevel	Dump level. The dump level is an integer (0...9) that is used to decide what files are backed up during incremental backups. A level 0 dump backs up all files on the filesystem. If a non-zero dump level is given, all files that were modified since the last dump level that was lower than the current level will be backed up. For example, a level 2 dump would back up all files that were modified since the last 1 or 0 backup.

continues >>

>>continued

Option	Description
file	Dump file. Backup is dumped to the specified file rather than to /dev/rmt/0.
l	Autoload. At the end of the tape, the drive is taken offline and waits two minutes before going back online. This allows autoloaders to perform correctly.
n	Notify. All users in the sys group are notified of any problems encountered during a backup.
o	Offline. The tape drive is taken offline after the backup is complete or the end of the tape is reached—whichever comes first.
S	Do not perform the backup—only print an estimate of the space needed to perform the dump.
s size	Specify the size of the backup device media (tapes). This option is not required. Values are given in feet and should be slightly less than the actual tape length.
t tracks	Specify the number of tracks for a cartridge tape. Not usually needed. The default value is 9.
u	Add an entry (filesystem name, date, dump level) to the /etc/dumpdates file.
v	Verify. Check the dumped filesystem against the backup copy.
w	Warn. Print filesystems that have not been backed up in more than a day.
W	Warn with highlight. Print all filesystems in /etc/ dumpdates, highlighting filesystems that have not been backed up in more than a day.

Restoring a Filesystem from a Backup (ufsrestore)

ufsrestore

The ufsrestore utility is used to restore filesystems from backups.

Backup Modes

Mode	Function Letter	Description
Extract	x	Extract the files specified from the media to the filesystem.

continues >>

Mode	Function Letter	Description
Interactive	i	The `ufsrestore` utility runs in interactive mode, prompting for responses from the user, after reading the initial information from the backup media. In this mode, commands can be used (given later in this section).
Recursive	r	Recursively restore an entire filesystem into the current top-level directory.
Resume	R	Resume restoring at a particular volume of a backup after it was interrupted.
Table-of-Contents	t	Print a table of contents of the backup media, showing all files.

Modifer	Description
a *file*	Use the table of contents in the specified file rather than from the backup media.
b *factor*	Blocking factor. Specify the blocking factor for a tape backup in 512-byte blocks.
c	Convert old format media to new `ufs` format.
d	Debug. Print debugging information.
f *file*	Use the file specified by *file* rather than /dev/rmt/0 as the source from which to restore.
h	Restore the actual directory from the backup rather than from the files referenced by it.
m	Restore by inode number rather than by filename.
s *n*	Extract from the backup media starting at the nth file.
v	Verbose. Show extra information when restoring from a backup.
y	Force `ufsrestore` to continue when errors are encountered.

Command	Description
add *file*	Add the specified file to the list of files to be extracted from the backup media.
cd *directory*	Change to the specified directory in the dump file.

continues >>

>>continued

Command	Description
delete *file*	Delete the specified file (or directory) from the list of files to be extracted from the backup media.
extract	Extract all files on list to be restored. The list is created using the add and delete commands.
help	Print a summary of commands.
ls	List files and directories in the current working directory in the dump file.
pwd	Print the current working directory.
quit	Exit immediately.
setmodes	Interactively ask for modes to set ".".
verbose	Toggle the verbose flag. If verbose is on, inode numbers are shown when the ls command is used.
what	Print the media dump header.

Copying Filesystems

Copying Volumes (volcopy)

volcopy   The volcopy command can be used by the root user to make a copy of a labeled filesystem. This command works with ufs filesystems, but may not work with other filesystem types. Unless the -a option is specified on the command line, the volcopy utility will pause 10 seconds before making the copy.

Use dd for Copying to Tape Devices

Use the volcopy utility for copying between disks. To copy a volume to a tape device, use the dd utility.

Option	Description
-a	Prompt the user for confirmation before copy is made.
-F *type*	Specify the filesystem type.
-o *options*	Specify filesystem-specific options as a comma-delimited list.
-V	Print the command line but do not perform any actions.

Copying and Converting Files (cpio, dd)

Two main utilities exist to copy and convert files or entire filesystems. The   cpio, dd
cpio utility is used to copy file archives, and the dd utility is used to copy
and convert files (to tape drives, especially). The cpio utility preserves file
modes and permissions.

cpio Mode	Mode Letter	Description
Copy In	-i	Read from standard input, creating the extracted files and directories and preserving file modes and permissions. If the user is the root user, file user and group ownerships will be preserved as well.
Copy Out	-o	Read from standard input to create a list of files and paths to copy. This information is sent to standard output along with path and status information.
Pass	-p	Read a list of pathnames and copy the associated files and directories to the specified destination.

Option	Description
-a	Reset access times of copied files.
-A	Add files to an archive file.
-B	Block input and output to 5,120 bytes per record.
-c	Keep header information in ASCII format when reading or writing.
-C size	Set the input/output buffer size to size. The default buffer size is 512 bytes.
-d	Directories are created if needed.
-E file	Read filenames to be copied from the specified file.
-H header	Set the header format to header. Valid header values are Bar, crc, odc, tar, and ustar.
-I file	Treat the specified file as an input file, reading filenames from the file. The file can also be a special device.

continues >>

>>continued

Option	Description
-k	Skip corrupted file headers and continue.
-l	Link rather than copy files.
-L	Symbolic links are followed.
-m	Do not change file modification times.
-M *msg*	Define the message that is printed when it is time to change media when using the -O or -I option.
-O *file*	Send output of cpio to the specified file. The file can also be a special device.
-P	Preserve access control lists (ACLs).
-r	The user is prompted to rename each file as it is read.
-R *uid*	Interactively change the *uid* of each file. You must be the root user to do this.
-t	Print input table of contents.
-u	Unconditional copy. By default (without -u), older files will not replace newer files of the same name.
-v	Verbose. Print informational messages.
-V	Special Verbose. Print only files that are copied.

Example	Description
Find . -print ¦ cpio ➥-dump {output}	Copy one directory tree to another.

dd

An alternative to using cpio is dd, which can be used to copy and convert files. This utility is especially useful for copying to tape drives. The block size of input and output streams can be converted.

Operand	Description
bs=*n*	Set the output and input block sizes to the same value.
cbs=*n*	Set the conversion block size. Only used with ASCII and EBCDIC conversions.
conv= *conversion*	Convert the input using the specified conversion format. Conversions are given in the subsequent table.

continues >>

Operand	Description
count=*n*	Copy *n* input blocks.
files=*n*	Copy *n* files before exiting.
ibs=*n*	Set the input block size.
if=*file*	Use *file* as the input path. The default value is standard input.
iseek=*n*	Seek, rather than skip, *n* blocks of the input file before copying and converting (faster than skipping for disk files).
obs=*n*	Set the output block size.
of=*file*	Use *file* as the out path. The default value is standard output.
oseek=*n*	Seek, rather than skip, *n* blocks from the beginning of the output file before copying.
skip=*n*	Skip *n* blocks and then begin to copy and convert.

Conversions

Option	Description
ascii	EBCDIC to ASCII conversion.
block	Treat newlines as the end of records rather than depending on block lengths.
ebcdic	ASCII to EBCDIC conversion.
ibm	Different ASCII to EBCDIC.
lcase	Uppercase to lowercase conversion.
noerror	Do not stop if an error occurs.
notrunc	Do not truncate the output file.
swab	If the number of bytes in the input record is odd, ignore the last byte.
sync	Input blocks are made to be the size of ibs=*buffer* by appending null characters.
ucase	Lowercase to uppercase conversion.
unblock	Fixed-length to variable-length conversion. Remove trailing spaces and add terminating newlines.

Example	Description
dd if=/dev/rmt/0 of= ➥outfile conv=ebcdic	Convert an ASCII tape to an EBCDIC file.
dd if=/dev/rmt/0 of=/ ➥dev/rmt/.1	Copy from one tape drive to another.

▶ **See Also** tar (204)

Creating and Extracting Tape Archives (tar)

tar   /usr/bin/tar [*options*] [*function*][*modifier*] [*tarfile*] [*file*]

One common way to transmit and store files is as a tape archive, commonly called a *tar file*. Traditionally, tar files were magnetic tape files; however, tar files can now be any file on any filesystem. Most source code is distributed as a compressed tar file. tar files usually have a .tar filename extension. The tar command is used to create, list, and extract tar files.

Option	Description
-C *dir file*	Use the chdir command on the directory specified by *dir*. Then create a tar file pecified by *file*.
-I *file*	Use a file containing a list of filenames and run the tar command line on each filename. Do not leave any trailing space characters at he end of each line. Do not leave any blank lines at the end of the file.

Function Letter	Description
c	Create. Create a new tar file archive.
r	Replace. Write the new files to the end of the existing specified file.
t	Table of Contents. Print a listing of all of the filenames and pathnames for the tar file.
u	Update. The specified files to be added to the tar file are appended to the end of the file if and only if they are not already in the tar file. This process is slow.
x	Extract. The files stored in the tape archive are extracted. The tar file can contain directory names. Any directory names not already existing on the system and specified in the tar file will be created. It is recommended that a table of contents be printed before extracting files to check where they will be extracted to.

Solaris 1.x and 2.x Incompatibilities When Using tar

It should be noted that the update function (u) depends on the system on which the tar file was created. If the tar file was created on a Solaris 1.x system, it can be updated only on a Solaris 1.x system. If the tar file was created on a Solaris 2.x system, it can be updated only on a Solaris 2.x system.

Function Modifier	Description
b	Blocking Factor. Specify the blocking factor (in 512-byte blocks) for writing to raw magnetic devices.
B	Block. Read multiple times when reading from standard input or across an ethernet.
e	Error. If an error occurs, exit immediately.
f	Filename. Specify a filename rather than a device name. This is used when creating a new tar file.
F	Exclude all directories named SCCS and RCS.
FF	Exclude all directories named SCCS and RCS and all files ending in .o.
h	Treat symbolic links as files and follow them.
i	Ignore checksum errors.
l	Link-Error. Print error messages in the event a link cannot be resolved.
m	Modify. When used with the extract function, the modification time of the tar file is set to the time of the last extraction.
number	Specify the drive number for the tape drive. This value must be a number between 0 and 7. The default drive number is stored in /etc/default/tar.
o	Set the ownership of the extracted files to the user running the tar command.
p	Keep the original file modes and permissions of the files in the tar archive when extracting files.
P	Do not add a trailing slash to directory names.
v	Verbose. Print extra information when running, especially when printing the table of contents.

continues >>

>>continued

Function Modifier	Description
w	Confirm the requisition function. The user must respond with a single y to confirm and continue.
X	Exclude. Specify a text file containing a list of files to exclude from being placed in a new tar file or extracted from an existing tar file. When used with the t function, the file-names will not be printed.

Example	Task
tar vxf source.tar	Extract the files from the tape archive called source.tar, showing all files extracted.
tar cvf source.tar ./dev	Create a tar file called source.tar, including all the files and pathnames in the dev subdirectory.

▶ **See Also** "Copying and Converting Files (cpio, dd)," (201)

10
Security

System Auditing

Enabling the Basic Security Module (BSM)

BSM   The Solaris Basic Security Module (BSM) is enabled or disabled on a system by using two scripts in the /etc/security directory. The BSM increases the security of a system in many respects.

Action	Command
Enable BSM	/etc/security/bsmconv
Disable BSM	/etc/security/bsmunconv

Executing bsmconv with no options or arguments will enable the BSM on the host machine as well as any diskless clients being served by the host machine. It is important to reboot after enabling the BSM.

The BSM must be enabled to use any of the Solaris auditing facilities.

Diskless clients can enable the BSM by running bsmconv on the server system and specifying the exported root directory.

Example	Task
bsmconv	Enable the BSM on the local host and all diskless clients supported by the host.
bsmconv /export/root/ ➥host3	Enable the BSM on the diskless client called host3.

Third-Party Tools

Third-Party
Tools

Some third-party tools may provide similar or better security. Some of these security tools (most are freeware) to consider are summarized in the following sections.

COPS

ftp://coast.cs.purdue.edu/pub/tools/unix/cops/1.04/

The Computer Oracle and Password System (COPS) is a proactive security tool for UNIX systems. It checks the local system for common security flaws and weaknesses and then reports them. Suggestions are given for fixing the problems, or the problems can be automatically fixed.

Internet Security Scanner (ISS)

```
http://www.iss.net
```

Much like COPS, this is a proactive security tool that attempts to "crack" the system. This tool can, however, be used to check remote systems. In many ways this is similar to the SATAN tool that was released (and gained much media hype). New versions of the ISS security tools have a very nice graphical user interface.

TAMU Tiger

```
ftp://coast.cs.purdue.edu/pub/tools/unix/TAMU/
```

The TAMU Tiger scripts from Texas A&M University are Perl scripts that perform security checks on UNIX systems. It works, in many ways, like COPS. The scripts are extremely easy to use and configure. Tiger is a good security check to run on a regular basis.

Tripwire

```
ftp://coast.cs.purdue.edu/pub/tools/unix/Tripwire/
```

The Tripwire program creates digital signatures of selected and important files, routinely checking the signatures against new checksums. If a difference is found, it means that an intruder has changed one of the files and the system administrator is notified. This program may not be necessary for most systems, but it does increase the security of the system.

Starting the Auditing System

The `audit_startup` script must be executed before the audit daemon (`auditd`) is started. The script is located at

Starting the Auditing System

```
/etc/security/audit_startup
```

It is available only after the Solaris BSM has been enabled using the `bsmconv` script.

The `audit_startup` script is a plain text file and can be manually edited by the system administrator.

Example

Use the following to initialize the audit system:

```
audit_startup
```

The Audit Daemon

The Audit daemon can be used only after the Solaris Basic Security Module has been enabled using the bsmconv script. After the BSM has been enabled, the Audit daemon will generate audit trail files, which can be used to enhance the security of a system. The Audit daemon is controlled through the audit control file (/etc/security/audit/ audit_control).

The daemon will use the audit_warn utility to warn of potential problems under the following conditions.

Auditing Condition	Description
allhard	All filesystems are full or are unavailable. No audit trail files will be written. Warnings will be issued every 20 seconds.
allsoft	All filesystems have exceeded their minimum free space requirements. A new audit trail will be created anyway.
auditoff	The Audit daemon has exited.
ebusy	An Audit daemon is already running.
getacdir	A problem with the directory list in /etc/security/audit/ audit_control has been found. The Audit daemon will wait until this problem has been corrected.
hard	A filesystem has become full or is unable to be written to. A new Audit trail will be created on a different filesystem if possible.
nostart	The Audit daemon cannot be started. Reboot and try again.
postsigterm	A problem was encountered while attempting to shut down the Audit daemon.
soft	A filesystem minimum free space limit has been exceeded. A new audit trail file will be created on a different file system.
tmpfile	A temporary audit file already exists. This indicated that the daemon was not properly shut down the last time it was run.

Current Audit daemon information is stored in a file in ./etc/security called audit_data. The /etc/security/audit_data file has the following format:

```
pid:logpath
```

pid is the Audit daemon process identification number, and logpath is the path and filename of the Audit daemon log file.

Printing Audit Trail Files

Audit log files are commonly called *audit trail files*. They contain information gathered by the Audit daemon as specified in the /etc/security/audit_control file. The location of the audit trail files is defined in the audit_control file using the dir: lines.

Printing Audit Trail Files

Audit trail files must be read using the praudit utility. If no filename is given, the input from standard input is assumed to be in the format of an audit trail file. Up to 100 audit trail files can be listed on the command line for printing.

Option	Description
-dchar	Use the character specified by char as the delimiter.
-1	Print one line per record.
-r	Print records in raw format. All times, ID numbers, and events are shown as integers.
-s	Print records in short format. All times, ID numbers, and events are converted to a readable ASCII format.

Task	Example
praudit -r audit001	Print the audit trail file called audit001 in raw format.
praudit -s audit002	Print the audit trail file called audit002, converting to ASCII format.

Audit Warnings

Audit warnings are handled by the audit_warn script. These warnings are sent from the Audit daemon (auditd). Also, users can be specified as audit_warn in the mail aliases file. These users will receive email concerning any warnings.

Audit Warnings

Warning	Description	Default Action
allhard count	The hard limit for all filesystems has been exceeded the number of times specified by count.	Send mail to the audit_warn alias the first time the warning is logged (count=1). Write a message to the console every time.
allsoft	The soft limit for all filesystems has been exceeded.	Send mail to audit_warn alias and write a message to the console.
auditoff	The system audit state was changed from AUC_AUDITING by someone other than auditd.	Send mail to audit_warn alias and write a message to the console.
ebusy	The Audit daemon is already running.	Send mail to audit_warn alias and write a message to the console.
getacdir count	There is a problem with the directory list in the audit_control file.	Send mail to audit_warn alias the first time the message is logged. Write a message to the console every time.
hard filesystem	Hard limit for the filesystem has been exceeded.	Send mail to audit_warn alias and write a message to the console.
nostart	Auditing could not be started.	Send mail to audit_warn alias and write a message to the console.
postsigterm	The Audit daemon was improperly shut down.	Send mail to audit_warn alias and write a message to the console.
soft filesystem	The soft limit of a filesystem has been exceeded.	Send mail to audit_warn alias and write a message to the console.
tmpfile	The temporary audit file already exists. This is an indication of a previous error.	Send mail to audit_warn alias and write a message to the console.

Controlling the Audit Daemon

The Audit daemon (auditd) is controlled by editing the /etc/
security/audit_control file. The file is a plain text file and can be
edited manually. Comment lines begin with #, and are ignored.

Audit Parameter	audit_control Line	Description
Audit old	minfree:*percent*	Specify the minimum free thresh space. If the allowed free space goes below this amount, an audit_warn warning is sent.
Audit trail file directories	dir:*directory*	Specify the directory in which audit trail files will be written. More than one dir: line can be specified, in order of preference.
Flags	flags: *flags*	Define what events are audited. These flags can be overridden by the audit_user file.
Non-attributable flags	naflags: *flags*	Define what events are audited that cannot be associated with a specific user.

The Audit daemon can also be controlled to log specific events for
individual users on the system. This is done by adding lines to the
/etc/security/audit_user file. The format of the file is as follows:

    username:flags-to-audit:flags-not-to-audit

The audit_user file always overrides the audit_control file.

Event	Flag	Long Name
Access of object attributes	fa	file_attr_acc
Admin actions	ad	administrative
All	all	all
Application auditing	ap	application
Change of object attributes	fm	file_attr_mod

continues >>

>>continued

Event	Flag	Long Name
Creation of object	fc	file_creation
Deletion of object	fd	file_deletion
Everything else	ot	other
exec calls	ex	exec
File close	cl	file_close
ioctl calls	io	ioctl
IPC calls	ip	ipc
Login/logout	lo	login_logout
Network events	nt	network
Non-attributable events	na	non_attrib
Process operations	pc	process
Read of data, open for read	fr	file_read
Write of data, open for write	fw	file_write

Event Flag Modifers

Modifier	Description
-	Audit if event failed.
+	Audit only if event was successful.

Task	Example
dir: /etc/security/argus/ ➥auditdir: /etc/security/ ➥argus.aux/ audit	Set up directory to store audit trail files, as well as a backup directory.
flags: -fw	Audit all failed attempts to write to files.

ASET

Automated Security Enhancement Tool (ASET) Overview

```
aset [options]
```

Solaris comes with a built-in security tool called the Automated Security Enhancement Tool (ASET). ASET is a security suite that can be used to increase the general security of the system. It does not fix all security problems, but it can prevent some of the more common problems associated with the administration of Solaris systems.

ASET restricts access to important system files and directories. The amount of protection depends on the security level chosen when ASET is started. Specific definitions of what tasks are performed at each security level are stored in the `asetenv` and `aset` master files. Reports generated from ASET are stored in the `/usr/aset/reports` directory.

ASET Security Levels

Level	Description
low	No system changes are made. System security checks are performed and weaknesses are reported.
med	Some system changes are made to restrict access to key system files. System security checks are performed and weaknesses are reported.
high	Many system changes are made to restrict access to key system files and directories. Some applications and services may change in functionality due to increased security. System security checks are performed and weaknesses are reported.

Option	Description
-d *directory*	Set the working directory for the ASET system. This must be the directory in which ASET has been installed. The default value for the working directory is `/usr/aset`.
-l *level*	Specify the security level at which to run ASET. Valid levels include low, med, and high.
-n *user@host*	Mail the output of the ASET execution to the user specified. The output is in summary format.
-p	Run ASET periodically via the `cron` service. The time period is defined by the `PERIODIC_SCHEDULE` environment variable in the `/usr/aset/asetenv` file.
-u *userlist*	Check the environments of the users listed in the file specified by *userlist*. By default, only the root account is checked.

ASET Tasks

Task	Description
cklist	A checksum is generated for specified system files the first time this task is executed. Subsequent executions compare the previous checksum against a new checksum generated from the file. Any inconsistencies (evidence that the file has been modified) are reported. This task can be customized by changing the ASET environment file CKLISTPATH parameters.
eeprom	Set the secure parameter on newer eeprom versions.
env	Check environment variables defined in .rc files for the root user (and any other users specified with the -u option). Common problems such as a dot in the PATH environment variable and UMASK problems are reported.
firewall	Set up the system to be used as a firewall (AKA bastion) host. IP forwarding is disabled, as well as other tasks to make the system more secure.
sysconf	Check system configuration files for common security problems. The following files are checked: ■ /etc/hosts.equiv ■ /etc/inetd.conf ■ /etc/aliases ■ /etc/default/login ■ /etc/vfstab ■ /etc/dfs/dfstab ■ /etc/ftpusers ■ /var/adm/utmp ■ /var/adm/utmpx ■ /.rhosts
tune	Increase security by setting more restrictive file permissions on system files. The amount and type of file permission changes can be customized by editing the ASET master files.
usrgrp	User accounts and groups are checked for common problems. This task is similar to the grpck and pwck commands.

▶ **See Also** ASET Environment File (217), ASET Masters (218)

ASET Environment File

/usr/aset/asetenv

The ASET environment file (/usr/aset/asetenv) is used to manually configure the Automatic Security Enhancement Tool. There are two types of parameters listed in the file: *User Configurable Parameters* and *ASET Internal Environment Variables*. Only the User Configurable Parameters should be changed.

ASET Parameter	Description
CKLISTPATH_ LOW CKLISTPATH_ MED CKLISTPATH_ HIGH	Set files to have checksums generated during a cklist task. Each security level can be individually customized.
PERIODIC_ SCHEDULE	Set how often period ASET checks are performed.
TASK	Set the tasks that will be performed by ASET. Valid tasks include the following: ■ tune: Restrict access to system files. ■ usrgrp: Perform checks on user account and group information. ■ sysconf: Perform checks on system configuration files. ■ env: Check user environment variables. ■ cklist: Perform checksum consistency checks. ■ eeprom: Set secure parameter for eeproms. ■ firewall: Set up system to be used as a firewall host.
UID_ALIASES	Set the filename for a file to define allowable duplicate UIDs.
YPCHECK	If this is set to true, NIS equivalents are checked as well.

Example

```
CKLISTPATH_HIGH=$CKLISTPATH_MED:/usr/lib:/usr/sbin
CKLISTPATH_LOW=/etc/:/
CKLISTPATH_MED=$CKLISTPATH_LOW:/usr/bin:/usr/ucb
PERIODIC_SCHEDULE="0 0 * * *"
TASKS="env sysconf usrgrp"
UID_ALIASES=/usr/aset/masters/uid_aliases
YPCHECK=false
```

Printing ASET Status

`/usr/aset/util/taskstat [options]`

The `taskstat` utility can be used to check the status of the Automatic Security Enhancement Tool (ASET) while it is running in the background. The output of `taskstat` shows a list of all security tasks being executed, noting which have been completed and which are still running. When all tasks have been completed, the report will be stored in `/usr/aset/reports`.

Option	Description
-d *directory*	Set the working directory for ASET.

ASET Masters

`/usr/aset/masters/`

The Automated Security Enhancement Tool (ASET) can be configured by editing the files in the `./usr/aset/masters` directory. By default the files are set to provide a reasonable amount of security and do not need to be modified. However, system administrators can edit the files to properly tune the ASET system.

Master File	Description
cklist.low cklist.med cklist.high	`cklist` task. The checksums generated by the `cklist` task are stored in these files. To configure the `cklist` task, consult the ASET master files.
tune.low tune.med tune.high	`tune` task. These files set the mode, owner, group, and type of the files specified. Three files exist, so each security level can be individually customized. The wildcard character (*) can be used in the `pathname` field. Valid types include `symlink`, `directory`, and `file`. Format: *pathname mode owner group type*
uid_alias	`usrgrp` task. Defines UIDs that can be duplicated for accounts. Usually duplicate UIDs are not allowed by ASET. This file can override that security check for specific UIDs. Format: *uid=username1=username2=username3=...*

ASET Restore

/usr/aset/aset.restore [*options*]

The aset.restore utility exists to undo all of the security enhancements made by the Automated Security Enhancement Tool (ASET). All files, file permissions, and other objects are returned to the same state they were before ASET was initially run. This is helpful if ASET removed the functionality of some part of the system while attempting to increase security.

Option	Description
-d *directory*	Specifies the ASET working directory. By default, the working directory is set to /usr/aset.

Network Sniffing

snoop

In many ways, network sniffers are used as system-cracking tools or network troubleshooting tools. However, it is good to understand network sniffing in order to have a firm grasp on the security of the system. The snoop utility comes with Solaris and provides a good way to learn about network sniffing.

Network packets can be captured and displayed using the Solaris snoop utility. The packets can be filtered, capturing only packets of interest. Several formats are available for displaying captured packets.

Option	Description
-a	Convert packets to audio using /dev/audio. This option is not very useful on a busy network.
-C	Print filter expression code.
-c *n*	Capture *n* packets and quit.
-D	Print the number of packets dropped in summary format.

continues >>

>>continued

Option	Description
-d *dev*	Capture packets from the device specified by *dev*. The default value is /dev/le0.
-i *file*	Read packets from the capture file specified by *file*.
-N	Create an IP/DNS-name mapping file that lists all IP addresses and associated names. Must be used with the -i option.
-n *file*	Use the file specified by *file* to convert IP addresses to names. The file must be of the following format: *ip-addr hostname*
-o *file*	Write captured packets to *file*.
-P	Non-promiscuous mode. Only show packets addressed to host (plus broadcast and multicast packets).
-p *list*	Display the packets specified in the comma-delimited *list*.
-S	Show Ethernet frame size.
-s *snaplength*	Capture only a part of packets. Packets are shortened to the specified *snaplength*.
-t *stamp*	Timestamp packets with one of three modes. The stamp is specified by *stamp*, which is one of the following: ■ r: Relative—Based on the time of the first packet ■ a: Absolute—Wall-clock time ■ d: Delta—Time between packets
-v	Verbose. Use extra detail when displaying packets, including full packet headers.
-V	Verbose Summary. More detail than normal mode, but less detail than verbose mode.
-x *offset*	Print packet contents in hex and ASCII format, using *offset* as the offset. An offset of 0 will print the entire packet.

Filter Expressions

Expression	Description
apple	Print all Apple Ethertalk packets.
broadcast	Print all broadcast packets.
decnet	Print all DECNET packets.
ether	Resolve hosts to Ethernet addresses.
etheraddr	Print all packets that have etheraddr as their source or destination Ethernet address (such as aa:0:54:53:65:23). A zero (0) must be prepended to the Ethernet address.
ethertype n	Print packets that have n as the Ethernet type field number.
from	Can be added to host, net, ipaddr, etheraddr, port, or rpc to specify that the packet must be from that expression (source).
gateway host	Print all packets that used the specified host as a gateway.
greater length	Print all packets longer than length.
host hostname	Print packets with hostname as their source address.
ipaddr	Print all packets with ipaddr as their source or destination.
less length	Print all packets smaller than length.
multicast	Print all multicast packets.
net net	Print all packets to or from the specified network number.
nofrag	Print only unfragmented packets.
packet-type	Print all packets of a specific type. This can be one of three types: ip, arp, rarp.
port port	Print all packets to or from the specified port number.
protocol	Print all packets of a specific protocol type: udp, tcp, icmp.
rpc prog	Print all packets to or from the specified RPC program.
to	Can be added to host, net, ipaddr, etheraddr, port, or rpc to specify what the packet must be to that expression (destination).

Kerberos

Kerberos Overview

The Kerberos authentication and authorization system can be used for increased security on a computer network. Once logged into the system, users can authenticate themselves with the Kerberos daemon and then use the Kerberos functions of services (such as NFS). A major advantage of using Kerberos is that once authenticated, .rhosts are no longer needed for services such as rlogin and rsh. Users must first be registered with the Kerberos system before they can properly use it; the system administrator must perform this registration task. Once registered, users log in to the Kerberos system using the kinit command.

Kerberos Name Parts

Part	Description
Principal name	The user's username or the service name
Instance	For users, this is NULL. For services, this is the name of the machine that the service is running on.
Realm	The service providing authentication for the principal.

Once authenticated, the user or service is given a *Kerberos ticket*, an encrypted protocol that can be used for authentication. These tickets expire after a predetermined amount of time. After they expire, new tickets can be issued by re-running the kinit command.

Kerberos Daemon (kerbd)

The Kerberos daemon (kerbd) is the process that controls the entire Kerberos system by creating and validating tickets for kernel remote procedure calls. The daemon works between the kernel RPC calls and the key distribution center (KDC). The daemon is automatically started in normal multiuser run states.

Option	Description
-d	Debug. Extra output will be provided concerning ticket generation and validation.
-g	Do not initialize the grouplist. Only the group in the password file (/etc/passwd) for each use will be used in mapped credentials.

Configuring Kerberos

/etc/krb.conf

The Kerberos system can be configured by editing the Kerberos configuration file (/etc/krb.conf). This file stores information about Kerberos realms and key distribution centers (KDCs). The Kerberos daemon (kerbd) must be restarted whenever the Kerberos configuration file is changed.

```
local-realm-name
realm-name  realm-KDC-host
realm-name  realm-KDC-host
realm-name  realm-KDC-host
```

Administrative databases can be specified by adding admin server to the end of the realm lines in the file.

Kerberos realms File

The Kerberos system must translate hostnames to the corresponding realm name for each service provided by the host. This is done using the /etc/krb.realms file. Domain names must begin with a leading dot, such as the following:

```
.cs.university.edu
```

File Format

```
hostname    kerberos-realm
domainname  kerberos-realm
```

The following table elaborates on the file format and the conditions that can be met.

Condition	Result
hostname matches *hostname* field.	Kerberos realm of the matching field is used.
hostname does not match any *hostname* field, but domain name matches a *domainname* field.	Kerberos realm of the matching domain name field is used.
hostname does not match any *hostname* field, and domain name does not match any field.	The host's domain name (uppercase) is used as the realm *domainname*.

Logging In to the Kerberos Authentication System

kinit [*options*] [*username*]

Initialize and log in to the Kerberos authentication system. Before logging in, the user must first be registered with the Kerberos system. Running kinit will prompt the user for a username and password, unless the username is given on the command line. Once the user is logged in, a ticket-granting ticket will be created in /tmp for the user. The location of this ticket can be changed by putting a different path/filename in the KRBTKFILE environment variable. The ticket expires in eight hours.

To destroy tickets at any time after logging in, use the kdestroy command. See the section titled "Destroying Kerberos Tickets" for more information.

Option	Description
-I	Prompt the user for a Kerberos instance.
-l	Prompt the user for a ticket lifetime. Times are given in minutes and must be between 5 and 1,275 minutes and will be rounded to the closest multiple of 5. The default lifetime is 8 hours.
-r	Prompt the user for a Kerberos realm to authenticate with a remote server.
-v	Verbose. Print status messages.

Listing Kerberos Tickets

It is possible to list all tickets in a user's ticket file by using the `klist` utility. The ticket principal identity, principal names of all tickets, issue times, and expire times for all tickets will be printed. The `KRBTKFILE` environment variable is consulted to find the ticket file. If this variable is not set, the `/tmp` directory is checked for a ticket file for the user.

Option	Description
`-file file`	Use the file specified by `file` as the user ticket file.
`-s`	Silent. Only output the principal names of user tickets.
`-srvtab`	Treat the ticket file like a service key file.
`-t`	Check for a non-expired ticket-granting ticket. The exit status returns the results: ■ `1`: Ticket exists ■ `0`: No ticket exists

Retrieving a Ticket-Granting Ticket

```
/usr/bin/ksrvgt name instance [realm]
```

The `ksrvgt` utility retrieves a ticket-granting ticket and stores it in the ticket cache. This is done in three steps, as follows.

1. A ticket with a five-minute lifetime is fetched for the principal.

2. The response is decrypted using the `/etc/srvtab` file.

3. The ticket is stored in the standard ticket cache.

Destroying Kerberos Tickets

```
/usr/bin/kdestroy [options]
```

The `kdestroy` utility is used to destroy the user's active Kerberos authorization tickets. This is accomplished by overwriting the ticket file with zeros and then deleting the file. Also, any Kerberos credentials stored in the kernel are removed. If, for some reason, `kdestroy` is unable to properly destroy the user ticket, a warning message will be displayed along with a terminal beep. Only the current ticket file is destroyed.

Other ticket files are not removed. Therefore, it is recommended that all tickets be kept in one file.

Option	Description
-f	Suppress status messages.
-n	Destroy tickets, but do not remove credentials from the kernel.
-q	Quiet. Do not beep the terminal if kdestroy fails to properly destroy the tickets.

Automatically Destroying Tickets

If the /usr/bin/kdestroy command is added to a user's .logout file, the tickets will automatically be destroyed when the user logs out of the system. This makes the user's Kerberos system slightly more secure. However, because all Kerberos credentials stored in the kernel are removed, it is possible that NFS operations started by the user will fail after the user logs out.

III

Appendices

A
Solaris Version Changes

Solaris 2.2

- AnswerBook access over networks
- Multithreaded Library Interface
- New interface for installation
- OpenWindows improvements
- Volume Management (automatically mounts removable media)
- XGL Runtime Environment
- XIL 1.0 Imaging Runtime Libraries

Solaris 2.3

- Asynchronous PPP
- Automatic mounting of filesystems
- Direct Xlib 3.0 (MIT DDX)
- Improved disk caching
- NIS+ Setup Scripts
- PEX Runtime Environment 3D graphics support
- POSIX 1003.2
- Serial Port Manager
- X11R5–based OpenWindows
- XGL Runtime Environment graphics API

Solaris 2.4

- Added four European, four Asian, Latin American Spanish, and U.S. English languages
- Direct Xlib 3.1 (DGA Drawable Interface and mutiple frame buffer support)
- Kodak PhotoCD support
- OSF/Motif Runtime Environment
- PEX 2.2 Runtime Environment 3D graphics API
- Graphical installation procedure
- Transparent Overlays API
- Wider range of hardware configurations
- XGL 3.1 Runtime Environment
- XIL 1.2 Imaging Library Runtime Environment

Solaris 2.5

- AdminTools and Solstice AdminSuite for managing systems in a network
- Better conformance to XCU4 and POSIX standards
- Enhanced hardware support
- Filesystem (UFS)-improved error detection, access control lists
- Improved compatibility with Solaris 1.x
- Improved PPP security
- Name Service Cache Daemon
- NFS v.3: NFS over TCP, NFS Lock Manager, X/Open Federated Naming
- NIS+ Password Aging
- PEX 3.0 Runtime Environment
- Proc Tools for detailed process management
- Telnet client, rlogind/telnetd improved
- Time-sharing workload performance enhancements
- XGL 3.2 Runtime Environment
- XIL 1.2.1 Runtime Environment

Solaris 2.5.164-bit KAIO

- Improved support for Ultra series of workstations
- Large UID support
- Support for up to 3.75GB of virtual memory

Solaris 2.6

- Additional languages, Unicode 2.0, and TrueType fonts
- Changeable system boot device
- Documentation via a Web browser (AnswerBook2)
- Dynamic host configuration protocol (DHCP) support added
- HotJava Web browser included
- Java Virtual Machine (JVM) included, integrating Solaris and Java
- Large file support (1TB)
- Network time protocol (NTP) support added
- Solaris Software Development Kit (SDK) included
- Variable length subnet masks
- Web browser-based installation tool for initial installation
- WebNFS for file access via the Web using the Network Filesystem protocol
- Year 2000-compliant (previous versions are not completely Y2K-compliant)

Solaris 7

- Free for non-commercial developer or educational use
- Support for 64-bit operating system
- SNMP support included
- Improved PPP software
- Unzip program included
- Integrated UFS logging

continues >>

>>*continued*

- Sendmail 8.9.1b
- Fully Year 2000-compliant
- Centralized software management
- New commands: `plimit`, `pkill`, `pgrep`, `traceroute`
- SACK—support of selective acknowledgements (RFC 2018)
- Special packages available for ISPs and PC interaction
- Upgraded directory name lookup cache
- Dedicated dump partitions for crashes
- BIND 8.1.2, including dynamic updates (RFC 2136)
- Improved priority memory paging
- Processes are allowed to have address spaces greater than 4GB

B
Common Startup Problems and Solutions

After initially installing Solaris on a new system, there are a few common problems that most people encounter within the first few hours or days. These problems, and their possible solutions, are listed below. Note that there may be other solutions in addition to the ones given.

Problem	Solution
Cannot create user home directories under /home.	Comment out /home line in /etc/auto_master by placing a # as the first character of the line.
	Run the /usr/sbin/automount program to make the change take effect.
	Note: If disk space is an issue, consider making /home a link to /export/home or some other directory instead.
Hostnames resolve correctly using /etc/hosts, but hostname lookups using DNS servers fail.	Edit the hosts: line in /etc/nsswitch.conf to read: hosts: files dns
	Note: Other name services such as NIS can be specified as well.
	Create a /etc/resolv.conf file with the following contents: domain domainname nameserver ipaddr nameserver ipaddr

continues >>

>>continued

Problem	Solution
	domainname is the domain name (such as sun.com) and *ipaddr* is the IP address of the nameserver. Other nameserver lines can be added to provide backup servers in the event the first server in the list cannot be contacted.
Some users cannot FTP to the host even though they can log properly via telnet. C compiler does not appear to work. Running cc gives an error similar to: `language optional software package not installed`. `Unable to perform keyword searches of the online manual pages using man -k`.	Check to make sure the user's shell is included in the /etc/shells file. If it is not listed, edit the file to add it. Sun Solaris does not ship with a compiler included. The SunPro C compiler can be ordered from Sun Microsystems, or the free GNU Gcc compiler can be down loaded from the Internet. The index files required to perform keyword searches are not automatically built. To build these files, use the following command: `catman -w -M directory` *directory* is the manual page directory—usually /usr/share/man.

C
Signals

Name	Value	Default	Event
SIGHUP	1	Exit	Hangup
SIGINT	2	Exit	Interrupt. This is the default signal sent by the kill command
SIGQUIT	3	Dump Core	Quit. SIGINT should always be sent to a process before sending a SIGQUIT
SIGILL	4	Dump Core	Illegal Instruction
SIGTRAP	5	Dump Core	Trace/Breakpoint Trap
SIGABRT	6	Dump Core	Abort
SIGEMT	7	Dump Core	Emulation Trap
SIGFPE	8	Dump Core	Arithmetic Exception
SIGKILL	9	Exit	Killed
SIGBUS	10	Dump Core	Bus Error
SIGSEGV	11	Dump Core	Segmentation Fault
SIGSYS	12	Dump Core	Bad System Call
SIGPIPE	13	Exit	Broken Pipe
SIGALRM	14	Exit	Alarm Clock
SIGTERM	15	Exit	Terminated
SIGUSR1	16	Exit	User Signal 1

continues >>

>>continued

Name	Value	Default	Event
SIGUSR2	17	Exit	User Signal 2
SIGCHLD	18	Ignore	Child Status Changed
SIGPWR	19	Ignore	Power Fail/Restart
SIGWINCH	20	Ignore	Window Size Change
SIGURG	21	Ignore	Urgent Socket Condition
SIGPOLL	22	Exit	Pollable Event
SIGSTOP	23	Stop	Stopped
SIGTSTP	24	Stop	User Stopped
SIGCONT	25	Ignore	Continued
SIGTTIN	26	Stop	TTY Input Stopped
SIGTTOU	27	Stop	TTY Output Stopped
SIGVTALRM	28	Exit	Virtual Timer Expired
SIGPROF	29	Exit	Profiling Timer Expired
SIGXCPU	30	Dump Core	CPU Time Limit Exceeded
SIGXFSZ	31	Dump Core	File Size Limit Exceeded
SIGWAITING	32	Ignore	Threads Wait Signal
SIGLWP	33	Ignore	Lightweight Process (LWP) Signal
SIGFREEZE	34	Ignore	Check Point Freeze
SIGTHAW	35	Ignore	Check Point Thaw
SIGCANCEL	36	Ignore	Cancellation Signal

Commonly Used Signals

Task	Signal
Kill a process and all processes started by it.	kill -9 *pid*
Restart a process.	kill -HUP *pid*
Kill all processes owned by the user smithj.	/usr/ucb/ps -aux ¦ grep smithj ¦ grep -v grep ¦ awk '{print$1}' ¦ xargs kill -9

D
Web
Resources

Administration and Management

Resource Name	Location
Frequently Asked Questions About Sun NVRAM/hostid	`http://www.squirrel.com/squirrel/` `sun-nvram-hostid.faq.html`
How to Get PPP Running Between a PC Running Windows and a Sun Workstation Running Solaris 2.x	`http://sun.icsnet.com/faq/` `ppp-windows-sun.html`
NIS+ Frequently Asked Questions	`http://www.eng.auburn.edu/users/` `rayh/solaris/NIS+_FAQ.html`
Printing Under Solaris	`http://tat.bchs.uh.edu/~skerl/` `sun-faq/PrintFAQ/printfaq.html`
Questions and Answers on OpenBoot	`http://www.sunworld.com/` `swol-10-1995/swol-10-openboot.html`
Solaris and PPP FAQ	`http://www.sunhelp.org/faq/` `sunppp.html`
Sun Administration FAQ	`http://www.sunhelp.org/faq/` `sunadm.html`
Sun Managers Summaries Archives	`http://www.latech.edu/sunman.html`
SunSolve Online Public Patch Access	`http://sunsolve.sun.com/sunsolve/` `pubpatches/patches.html`

continues >>

>>continued

Resource Name	Location
TADPOLE Tidbits 'n RDI Ramblings	http://meltdown.under-ground.com/~revolver/laptop/
Useful Tools for Sun Workstations and Solaris	http://www.squirrel.com/squirrel/sun-stuff.html
What are the tunable kernel parameters for Solaris 2?	http://www.sunworld.com/swol-01-1996/swol-01-perf.html
ZD Solaris Tip of the Week	http://www.zdtips.com/sun/sun-f.htm

Common Desktop Environment/OpenLook

Resource Name	Location
Colormap FAQ List	http://tarl.net/FAQ/ColormapFAQ.html
Common Desktop Environment FAQ	http://www.webslingerz.com/sburnett/cde/index.html
Open Look FAQs	http://step.polymtl.ca/~coyote/openlook/index.html

Developer Resources

Resource Name	Location
Access1 Technical Information	http://access1.sun.com/techroom.html
IPv6 Development	http://playground.sun.com/pub/solaris2-ipv6/html/
Solaris Developer Support Centre	http://opcom.sun.ca/
Sun Solaris ABI Tools	http://www.sun.com/software/dev-progs/abi/

Hardware

Resource Name	Location
Celeste's Tutorial on Solaris 2.x Modems and Terminals	`http://www.stokely.com/ unix.serial.port.resources/ tutorials.html`
Frame Buffer FAQ	`http://tarl.net/FAQ/ FrameBuffer.html`
How do I install my Zip Drive on a Sun Workstation?	`http://www.iomega.com/support/ doconuments/2019.html`
How to install an Iomega Jaz Drive on a Sun Workstation	`http://www.iomega.com/support/ documents/4019.html`
Pictures of Sun Hardware	`http://sunpics.datatrax.net/`
SparcBook FAQ	`http://www.caiw.nl/~hvdkooij/ SparcBook-FAQ.html`
Sun CD-ROM FAQ	`http://saturn.tlug.org/suncdfaq/`

Lists of Resources

Resource Name	Location
Solaris Central	`http://www.solariscentral.org/`
Solaris WWW Resources	`http://oak.ece.ul.ie/~griffini/ solaris.html`
Sun FAQs, Patches, & Other Information	`http://www.stokely.com/ unix.sysadm.resources/ faqs.sun.html`
SunHELP	`http://www.sunhelp.com/`
SunSITE	`http://metalab.unc.edu/`
SunWHERE	`http://www.sunworld.com/ sunwhere.html`

continues >>

>>continued

Resource Name	Location
The Sun Shack	http://lios.apana.org.au/~cdewick/sun_ark.html
The Suns at Home Page	http://www.net-kitchen.com/~sah/
The Unofficial Guide to Solaris	http://sun.icsnet.com
UNIX Guru UniverseSolaris Page	http://www.ugu.com/sui/ugu/show?I=solaris&F=1111111111&G=Y

Magazines (Online and Print)

Resource Name	Location
Inside Solaris	http://www.zdjournals.com/sun/
SunExpert	http://www.netline.com/sunex/
SunWorld	http://www.sunworld.com/

Online Documentation

Resource Name	Location
RTFM	http://sun.icsnet.com/rtfm.html
Sun Product Documentation	http://docs.sun.com

Security

Resource Name	Location
Computer Incident Advisory Capability (CIAC)	http://ciac.llnl.gov/
Free Sun Patches	http://sunsolve.Sun.COM/pub-cgi/us/pubpatchpage.pl

continues >>

Resource Name	Location
Passwd+	ftp://ftp.dartmouth.edu/pub/security/
Securing a Solaris 2 Machine	http://www-uxsup.csx.cam.ac.uk/security/solaris2.html
TAMU Tiger Security Scripts	ftp://coast.cs.purdue.edu/pub/tools/unix/TAMU/
TCP Wrappers	ftp://coast.cs.purdue.edu/pub/tools/unix/tcp_wrappers/
The Solaris Security FAQ	http://www.sunworld.com/common/security-faq.html

Software

Resource Name	Location
Access1 Sun Software Support	http://access1.sun.com/
CERT Coordination Center	http://www.cert.org
Crack - Proactive Password Security	ftp://coast.cs.purdue.edu/pub/tools/unix/crack/
Free Software from Sun Microsystems	http://www.sun.com/products-n-solutions/promotions.html
Solaris Porting Project (This site is an excellent place to find source code as well as precompiled binaries for most Sun freeware packages.)	http://www.sunfreeware.com
The "ready-to-go" Solaris Helpers Page	http://home1.swipnet.se/%7Ew-10694/helpers.html

Solaris x86

Resource Name	Location
Hardware Compatibility List	http://access1.sun.com/drivers/hcl/hcl.html
Solaris x86 FAQ	http://dan.carlsbad.ca.us/faqs/s86faq.html
Solaris x86 Software	http://www.sun.com/software/Products/x86.html

Y2K

Resource Name	Location
Sun's Year 2000 Information Site	http://www.sun.com/y2000/
Y2K Solaris 2.3 through Solaris 2.6 Patches	http://sunsolve.Sun.COM/pub-cgi/us/ent2html?enotify/15972

E
TCP/UDP
Port List

Some ports have certain security issues related to them. Ports marked as "disable" are a major security concern and should be disabled if at all possible (via inetd.conf). Ports marked as "log" are possible security issues, but can still be used if some form of logging functionality is added. The best way to do this is to use TCP Wrappers written by Wietse Venema. It allows TCP ports to be logged ("wrapped") via inetd. It also provides host- and user-based access control for TCP ports. It can be downloaded for free from the following URL:

```
ftp://coast.cs.purdue.edu/pub/tools/unix/tcp_wrappers/
```

TCP/UDP Ports by Service

Service	Port	Security
biff	512/udp	Disable unless used
chargen	19/tcp	Log
chargen	19/udp	
courier	530/tcp	
csnet-ns	105/tcp	
daytime	13/tcp	Log
daytime	13/udp	
discard	9/tcp	Log
discard	9/udp	
domain	53/udp	
domain	53/tcp	
dtspc	6112/tcp	
echo	7/tcp	Log
echo	7/udp	
exec	512/tcp	Disable unless necessary
finger	79/tcp	Disable
fs	7100/tcp	
ftp	21/tcp	Log
ftp-data	20/tcp	
hostnames	101/tcp	
ident	113/tcp	Wrap
imap	143/tcp	Disable unless used
ingreslock	1524/tcp	Disable
iso-tsap	102/tcp	
kerberos	750/udp	
kerberos	750/tcp	
link	87/tcp	
listen	2766/tcp	
lockd	4045/udp	
lockd	4045/tcp	
login	513/tcp	
monitor	561/udp	
name	42/udp	
netstat	15/tcp	Disable
new-rwho	550/udp	Disable

Service	Port	Security
news	144/tcp	Disable
nfsd	2049/udp	
nfsd	2049/tcp	
nntp	119/tcp	
ntalk	518/udp	
ntp	123/tcp	
ntp	123/udp	
pcserver	600/tcp	
pop-2	109/tcp	Log
pop3	110/tcp	Log
printer	515/tcp	
rje	77/tcp	
rmonitor	560/udp	Disable
route	520/udp	
shell	514/tcp	Disable unless necessary
smtp	25/tcp	Log
sunrpc	111/udp	
sunrpc	111/tcp	
supdup	95/tcp	
syslog	514/udp	
systat	11/tcp	
talk	517/udp	
tcpmux	1/tcp	
telnet	23/tcp	Consider using ssh instead
tftp	69/udp	Disable
time	37/tcp	Log
time	37/udp	
ufsd	1008/tcp	
ufsd	1008/udp	
uucp	540/tcp	Disable
uucp-path	117/tcp	Disable
who	513/udp	Disable
whois	43/tcp	Disable
x400	103/tcp	
x400-snd	104/tcp	

TCP/UDP Ports by Port

Service	Port	TCP/UDP	Service	Port	TCP/UDP
tcpmux	1	/tcp	ident	113	/tcp
echo	7	/tcp	uucp-path	117	/tcp
echo	7	/udp	nntp	119	/tcp
discard	9	/tcp	ntp	123	/tcp
discard	9	/udp	ntp	123	/udp
systat	11	/tcp	imap	143	/tcp
daytime	13	/tcp	news	144	/tcp
daytime	13	/udp	exec	512	/tcp
netstat	15	/tcp	biff	512	/udp
chargen	19	/tcp	login	513	/tcp
chargen	19	/udp	who	513	/udp
ftp-data	20	/tcp	shell	514	/tcp
ftp	21	/tcp	syslog	514	/udp
telnet	23	/tcp	printer	515	/tcp
smtp	25	/tcp	talk	517	/udp
time	37	/tcp	ntalk	518	/udp
time	37	/udp	route	520	/udp
name	42	/udp	courier	530	/tcp
whois	43	/tcp	uucp	540	/tcp
domain	53	/udp	new-rwho	550	/udp
domain	53	/tcp	rmonitor	560	/udp
tftp	69	/udp	monitor	561	/udp
rje	77	/tcp	pcserver	600	/tcp
finger	79	/tcp	kerberos	750	/udp kdc
link	87	/tcp	kerberos	750	/tcp
supdup	95	/tcp	ufsd	1008	/tcp
hostnames	101	/tcp	ufsd	1008	/udp
iso-tsap	102	/tcp	ingreslock	1524	/tcp
x400	103	/tcp	nfsd	2049	/udp
x400-snd	104	/tcp	nfsd	2049	/tcp
csnet-ns	105	/tcp	listen	2766	/tcp
pop-2	109	/tcp	lockd	4045	/udp
pop3	110	/tcp	lockd	4045	/tcp
sunrpc	111	/udp	dtspc	6112	/tcp
sunrpc	111	/tcp	fs	7100	/tcp

Index

Symbols

* (asterisk), 56
/ filesystem, 178-180
< (less than), 46
¦ (pipe), 45

A

accounts, users
deleting, 162
locking, 163
modifying, 160

action, inittab, 152-153

actions
awk commands, 19
nawk commands, 28-31

adding
devices, 101
entries, mount command, 123
line numbers, nl command, 8
users, 158-160

administration and management Web sites, 237

advanced text tools
commands
awk, 19
grep, 27
ex commands, 21
nawk commands, 28
sed commands, 31

arguments
command-lines, 44
communications, write, 90

file transfers, rcp, 81
starting processes, at, 54

ASET (Automated Security Enhancement Tool), 214-215
environment file, 217
master files, 218
masters, 218
options, 215
restore utility, 219
security levels, 215
status, printing, 218
tasks, 216

ASET masters, files, 218

aset.restore utility, 219

at, 54

atq, starting processes, 55

atrm, starting processes, 55

audit control file, 211

Audit daemon
audit trail files, printing, 211
audit warnings, 211-212
auditing conditions, 210
controlling, 212-213
event flag modifers, controlling, 214

audit log files, 211

audit warnings, 212

auditing
conditions, Audit daemon, 210
systems, 209

Automated Security Enhancement Tool, *See* ASET

J

K

Q

R

Books for Networking Professionals

New Riders

Windows NT Titles

Windows NT TCP/IP

By Karanjit Siyan

1st Edition

480 pages, $29.99

ISBN: 1-56205-887-8

If you're still looking for good documentation on Microsoft TCP/IP, then look no further—this is your book. *Windows NT TCP/IP* cuts through the complexities and provides the most informative and complete reference book on Windows-based TCP/IP. Concepts essential to TCP/IP administration are explained thoroughly, then related to the practical use of Microsoft TCP/IP in a real-world networking environment. The book begins by covering TCP/IP architecture, advanced installation, and configuration issues, then moves on to routing with TCP/IP, DHCP Management, and WINS/DNS Name Resolution.

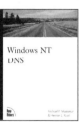

Windows NT DNS

By Michael Masterson, Herman L. Knief, Scott Vinick, and Eric Roul

1st Edition

340 pages, $29.99

ISBN: 1-56205-943-2

Have you ever opened a Windows NT book looking for detailed information about DNS only to discover that it doesn't even begin to scratch the surface? DNS is probably one of the most complicated subjects for NT administrators, and there are few books on the market that really address it in detail. This book answers your most complex DNS questions, focusing on the implementation of the Domain Name Service within Windows NT, treating it thoroughly from the viewpoint of an experienced Windows NT professional. Many detailed, real-world examples illustrate further the understanding of the material throughout. The book covers the details of how DNS functions within NT, then explores specific interactions with critical network components. Finally, proven procedures to design and set up DNS are demonstrated. You'll also find coverage of related topics, such as maintenance, security, and troubleshooting.

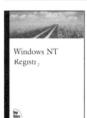

Windows NT Registry

By Sandra Osborne

1st Edition

564 pages, $29.99

ISBN: 1-56205-941-6

The NT Registry can be a very powerful tool for those capable of using it wisely. Unfortunately, there is very little information regarding the NT Registry, due to Microsoft's insistence that their source code be kept secret. If you're looking to optimize your use of the Registry, you're usually forced to search the Web for bits of information. This book is your resource. It covers critical issues and settings used for configuring network protocols, including NWLink, PTP, TCP/IP, and DHCP. This book approaches the material from a unique point of view, discussing the problems related to a particular component, and then discussing settings, which are the actual changes necessary for implementing robust solutions. There is also a comprehensive reference of Registry settings and commands, making this the perfect addition to your technical bookshelf.

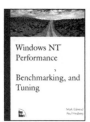

Windows NT Performance

By Mark Edmead and Paul Hinsberg
1st Edition
288 pages, $29.99
ISBN: 1-56205-942-4

Performance monitoring is a little like preventative medicine for the administrator: No one enjoys a checkup, but it's a good thing to do on a regular basis. This book helps you focus on the critical aspects of improving the performance of your NT system, showing you how to monitor the system, implement benchmarking, and tune your network. The book is organized by resource components, which makes it easy to use as a reference tool.

Windows NT Terminal Server

By Ted Harwood
1st Edition
416 pages, $29.99
ISBN: 1-56205-944-0

It's no surprise that most administration headaches revolve around integration with other networks and clients. This book addresses these types of real-world issues on a case-by-case basis, giving tools and advice for solving each problem. The author also offers the real nuts and bolts of thin client administration on multiple systems, covering such relevant issues as installation, configuration, network connection, management, and application distribution.

Windows NT Security

By Richard Puckett
1st Edition Fall 1999
600 pages, $29.99
ISBN: 1-56205-945-9

Swiss cheese. That's what some people say Windows NT security is like. And they may be right, because they only know what the NT documentation says about implementing security. Who has the time to research alternatives; play around with the features, service packs, hot fixes, and add-on tools; and figure out what makes NT rock solid? Well, Richard Puckett doe He's been researching Windows NT security for the University of Virginia for a while now, and he's got pretty good news. He's going to show you how to make NT secure in your environment, and we mean really secure.

Windows NT Network Management

By Anil Desai
1st Edition Spring 1999
400 pages, $34.99
ISBN: 1-56205-946-7

Administering a Window NT network is kind of like trying to herd cats—an impossible task characterized by constant motion, exhausting labor, and lot of hairballs. Author Anil Desai knows all about it—he's a Consulting Engineer for Sprint Paranet, and specializes in Window NT implementation, integration, and man agement. So we asked him to put togethe a concise manual of best practices, a book of tools and ideas that other administrator can turn to again and again in managing their own NT networks. His experience shines through as he shares his secrets for reducing your organization's Total Cost of Ownership.

Planning for Windows 2000

By Eric K. Cone
1st Edition Spring 1999
400 pages, $29.99
ISBN: 0-7357-0048-6

Windows 2000 is poised to be one of the largest and most important software releases of the next decade, and you are charged with planning, testing, and deploying it in your enterprise.

Are you ready? With this book, you will be. *Planning for Windows 2000* lets you know what the upgrade hurdles will be, informs you how to clear them, guides you through effective Active Directory design, and presents you with detailed roll-out procedures. Eric K. Cone gives you the benefit of his extensive experience as a Windows 2000 Rapid Deployment Program member, sharing problems and solutions he's encountered on the job.

MCSE Core NT Exams Essential Reference

By Matthew Shepker
1st Edition
256 pages, $19.99
ISBN: 0-7357-0006-0

You're sitting in the first session of your Networking Essentials class and the instructor starts talking about RAS and you have no idea what that means. You think about raising your hand to ask about RAS, but you reconsider—you'd feel pretty foolish asking a question in front of all these people. You turn to your handy *MCSE Core NT Exams Essential Reference* and find a quick summary on Remote Access Services. Question answered. It's a couple months later and you're taking your Networking Essentials exam the next day. You're reviewing practice tests and you keep forgetting the maximum lengths for the various commonly used cable types. Once again, you turn to the *MCSE Core NT Exams Essential Reference* and find a table on cables, including all of the characteristics you need to memorize in order to pass the test.

BackOffice Titles

Implementing Exchange Server

By Doug Hauger, Marywynne Leon, and William C. Wade III
1st Edition
400 pages, $29.99
ISBN: 1-56205-931-9

If you're interested in connectivity and maintenance issues for Exchange Server, then this book is for you. Exchange's power lies in its ability to be connected to multiple email subsystems to create a "universal email backbone." It's not unusual to have several different and complex systems all connected via email gateways, including Lotus Notes or cc:Mail, Microsoft Mail, legacy mainframe systems, and Internet mail. This book covers all of the problems and issues associated with getting an integrated system running smoothly and addresses troubleshooting and diagnosis of email problems with an eye towards prevention and best practices.

Exchange Server Administration

By Janice K. Howd
1st Edition Spring 1999
350 pages, $34.99
ISBN: 0-7357-0081-8

OK, you've got your Exchange Server installed and connected, now what? Email administration is one of the most critical networking jobs, and Exchange can be particularly troublesome in large, heterogenous environments. So Janice Howd, a noted consultant and teacher with over a decade of email administration experience, has put together this advanced, concise handbook for daily, periodic, and emergency administration. With in-depth coverage of topics like managing disk resources, replication, and disaster recovery, this is the one reference book every Exchange administrator needs.

SQL Server System Administration

By Sean Baird, Chris Miller, et al.

1st Edition

352 pages, $29.99

ISBN: 1-56205-955-6

How often does your SQL Server go down during the day when everyone wants to access the data? Do you spend most of your time being a "report monkey" for your co-workers and bosses? *SQL Server System Administration* helps you keep data consistently available to your users. This book omits the introductory information. The authors don't spend time explaining queries and how they work. Instead they focus on the information that you can't get anywhere else, like how to choose the correct replication topology and achieve high availability of information.

Internet Information Server Administration

By Kelli Adam, et. al.

1st Edition Fall 1999

300 pages, $29.99

ISBN: 0-7357-0022-2

Are the new Internet technologies in Internet Information Server giving you headaches? Does protecting security on the Web take up all of your time? Then this is the book for you. With hands-on configuration training, advanced study of the new protocols in IIS, and detailed instructions on authenticating users with the new Certificate Server and implementing and managing the new e-commerce features, *Internet Information Server Administration* gives you the real-life solutions you need. This definitive resource also prepares you for the release of Windows 2000 by giving you detailed advice on working with Microsoft Management Console, which was first used by IIS.

SMS Administration

By Wayne Koop and Brian Steck

1st Edition Fall 1999

350 pages, $29.99

ISBN: 0-7357-0082-6

Microsoft's new version of its Systems Management Server (SMS) is starting to turn heads. While complex, it's allowing administrators to lower their total cost of ownership and more efficiently manage clients, applications and support operations. So if your organization is using or implementing SMS, you'll need some expert advice. Wayne Koop and Brian Steck can help you get the most bang for your buck, with insight, expert tips, and real-world examples. Brian and Wayne are consultants specializing in SMS, having worked with Microsoft on one of the most complex SMS rollouts in the world, involving 32 countries, 15 languages, and thousands of clients.

Unix/Linux Titles

Solaris Essential Reference

By John P. Mulligan

1st Edition

350 pages, $19.99

ISBN: 0-7357-0023-0

Looking for the fastest, easiest way to find the Solaris command you need? Need a few pointers on shell scripting? How about advanced administration tips and sound, practical expertise on security issues? Are you looking for trustworthy information about available third-party software packages that will enhance your operating system? Author John Mulligan— creator of the popular Unofficial Guide to Solaris Web site (sun.icsnet.com)— delivers all that and more in one attractive, easy-to-use reference book. With clear and concise instructions on how to perform important administration and management tasks and key information on powerful commands and advanced topics, *Solaris Essential Reference* is the reference you need when you know what you want to do and you just need to know how.

Linux System Administration

By M Carling and James T. Dennis
1st Edition Summer 1999
450 pages, $29.99
ISBN: 1-56205-934-3

As an administrator, you probably feel that most of your time and energy is spent in endless firefighting. If your network has become a fragile quilt of temporary patches and workarounds, then this book is for you. For example, have you had trouble sending or receiving your email lately? Are you looking for a way to keep your network running smoothly with enhanced performance? Are your users always hankering for more storage, more services, and more speed? *Linux System Administration* advises you on the many intricacies of maintaining a secure, stable system. In this definitive work, the author addresses all the issues related to system administration, from adding users and managing files permission to Internet services and Web hosting to recovery planning and security. This book fulfills the need for expert advice that will ensure a trouble-free Linux environment.

Linux Security

By John S. Flowers
1st Edition Summer 1999
400 pages, $29.99
ISBN: 0-7357-0035-4

New Riders is proud to offer the first book aimed specifically at Linux security issues. While there are a host of general UNIX security books, we thought it was time to address the practical needs of the Linux network. In this definitive work, author John Flowers takes a balanced approach to system security, from discussing topics like planning a secure environment to firewalls to utilizing security scripts. With comprehensive information on specific system compromises, and advice on how to prevent and repair them, this is one book that every Linux administrator should have on the shelf.

Developing Linux Applications

By Eric Harlow
1st Edition
400 pages, $34.99
ISBN: 0-7357-0021-4

We all know that Linux is one of the most powerful and solid operating systems in existence. And as the success of Linux grows, there is an increasing interest in developing applications with graphical user interfaces that really take advantage of the power of Linux. In this book, software developer Eric Harlow gives you an indispensable development handbook focusing on the GTK+ toolkit. More than an overview on the elements of application or GUI design, this is a hands-on book that delves deeply into the technology. With in-depth material on the various GUI programming tools and loads of examples, this book's unique focus will give you the information you need to design and launch professional-quality applications.

Linux Essential Reference

David "Hacksaw" Todd
1st Edition Fall 1999
400 pages, $19.99
ISBN: 0-7357-0852-5

This book is all about getting things done as quickly and efficiently as possible by providing a structured organization to the plethora of available Linux information. We can sum it up in one word: VALUE. This book has it all: concise instruction on how to perform key administration tasks; advanced information on configuration; shell scripting; hardware management; systems management; data tasks; automation; and tons of other useful information. All coupled with an unique navigational structure and a great price. This book truly provides groundbreaking information for the growing community of advanced Linux professionals.

Linux Firewalls

By Robert Ziegler
Summer 1999
400 pages, $29.99
ISBN: 0-7357-0900-9

New Riders is proud to offer the first book aimed specifically at Linux security issues. While there are a host of general UNIX security books, we think it is time to address the practical needs of the Linux network. Author Robert Ziegler takes a balanced approach to system security, discussing topics like planning a secure environment, firewalls, and utilizing securtiy scripts. With comprehensive information on specific system compromises, and advice on how to prevent and repair them, this is one book that every Linux administrator should have on their shelf.

Development Titles

GTK+/Gnome Development

By Havoc Pennington
Summer 1999
400 pages, $29.99
ISBN: 0-7357-0078-8

GTK+ /Gnome Develpment provides the experienced programmer the knowledge to develop X Window applications with the powerful GTK+ toolkit. The author provides the reader with a checklist of features every application should have, advanced GUI techniques, and the ability to create custom widgets. The title also contains reference information for more experienced users already familiar with usage, but require knowledge of function prototypes and detailed descriptions. These tools let the reader write powerful applications in record time.

Python Essential Reference

By David Beazley
Fall 1999
270 pages, $19.99
ISBN: 0-7357-0901-7

This book describes the Python programming language and its library of standard modules. Python is an informal language that has become a highly valuable software development tool for many computing professionals. This language reference covers Python's lexical conventions, built-in datatypes, control flow, functions, statements, classes, and execution model. This book also covers the contents of the Python library as bundled in the standard Python distribution.

Lotus Notes and Domino Titles

Domino System Administration

By Rob Kirkland

1st Edition Fall 1999

500 pages, $29.99

ISBN: 1-56205-948-3

Your boss has just announced that you will be upgrading to the newest version of Notes and Domino when it ships. As a Premium Lotus Business Partner, Lotus has offered a substantial price break to keep your company away from Microsoft's Exchange Server. How are you supposed to get this new system installed, configured, and rolled out to all of your end users? You understand how Lotus Notes works—you've been administering it for years. What you need is a concise, practical explanation about the new features, and how to make some of the advanced stuff really work. You need answers and solutions from someone like you, who has worked with the product for years, and understands what it is you need to know. *Domino System Administration* is the answer—the first book on Domino that attacks the technology at the professional level, with practical, hands-on assistance to get Domino running in your organization.

Lotus Notes and Domino Essential Reference

By Dave Hatter & Tim Bankes

1st Edition

500 pages, $29.99

ISBN: 0-7357-0007-9

You're in a bind because you've been asked to design and program a new database in Notes for an important client that will keep track of and itemize a myriad of inventory and shipping data. The client wants a user-friendly interface, without sacrificing speed or functionality. You are experienced (and could develop this app in your sleep), but feel that you need to take your talents to the next level. You need something to facilitate your creative and technical abilities, something to perfect your programming skills. Your answer is waiting for you: *Lotus Notes and Domino Essential Reference*. It's compact and simply designed. It's loaded with information. All of the objects, classes, functions, and methods are listed. It shows you the object hierarchy and the overlaying relationship between each one. It's perfect for you. Problem solved.

Networking Titles

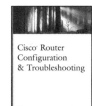

Cisco Router Configuration and Troubleshooting

By Mark Tripod

1st Edition

300 pages, $34.99

ISBN: 0-7357-0024-9

Want the real story on making your Cisco routers run like a dream? Why not pick up a copy of *Cisco Router Configuration and Troubleshooting* and see what Mark Tripod has to say? His company is the one responsible for making some of the largest sites on the Net scream, like Amazon.com, Hotmail, USAToday, Geocities, and Sony. In this book, he provides advanced configuration issues, sprinkled with advice and preferred practices. You won't see a general overview on TCP/IP—we talk about more meaty issues like security, monitoring, traffic management, and more. In the troubleshooting section, Mark provides a unique methodology and lots of sample problems to illustrate. By providing real-world insight and examples instead of rehashing Cisco's documentation, Mark gives network administrators information they can start using today.

Implementing Virtual Private Networks

By Tina Bird and Ted Stockwell

1st Edition Summer 1999
300 pages, $29.99
ISBN: 0-7357-0047-8

Tired of looking for decent, practical, up-to-date information on virtual private networks? *Implementing Virtual Private Networks,* by noted authorities Dr. Tina Bird and Ted Stockwell, finally gives you what you need—an authoritative guide on the design, implementation, and maintenance of Internet-based access to private networks. This book focuses on real-world solutions, demonstrating how the choice of VPN architecture should align with an organization's business and technological requirements. Tina and Ted give you the information you need to determine whether a VPN is right for your organization, select the VPN that suits your needs, and design and implement the VPN you have chosen.

Understanding Data Communications, Sixth Edition

By Gilbert Held

6th Edition Summer 1999
550 pages, $34.99
ISBN: 0-7357-0036-2

Updated from the highly successful fifth edition, this book explains how data communications systems and their variou[s] hardware and software components work Not an entry-level book, it approaches the material in a textbook format, addressing the complex issues involved in internetworking today. A great reference book for the experienced networking professional, written by noted networking authority, Gilbert Held.

New Riders

We Want to Know What You Think

To better serve you, we would like your opinion on the content and quality of this book. Please complete this card and mail it to us or fax it to 317-581-4663.

Name_____

Address _____

City _____ State _____ Zip _____

Phone _____

Email Address _____

Occupation _____

Operating System(s) that you use _____

What influenced your purchase of this book?
- ❑ Recommendation
- ❑ Table of Contents
- ❑ Magazine Review
- ❑ New Riders' Reputation
- ❑ Cover Design
- ❑ Index
- ❑ Advertisement
- ❑ Author Name

How would you rate the contents of this book?
- ❑ Excellent
- ❑ Good
- ❑ Below Average
- ❑ Very Good
- ❑ Fair
- ❑ Poor

How do you plan to use this book?
- ❑ Quick reference
- ❑ Classroom
- ❑ Self-training
- ❑ Other

What do you like most about this book?
Check all that apply.
- ❑ Content
- ❑ Accuracy
- ❑ Listings
- ❑ Index
- ❑ Price
- ❑ Writing Style
- ❑ Examples
- ❑ Design
- ❑ Page Count
- ❑ Illustrations

What do you like least about this book?
Check all that apply.
- ❑ Content
- ❑ Accuracy
- ❑ Listings
- ❑ Index
- ❑ Price
- ❑ Writing Style
- ❑ Examples
- ❑ Design
- ❑ Page Count
- ❑ Illustrations

What would be a useful follow-up book to this one for you? _____

Where did you purchase this book? _____

Can you name a similar book that you like better than this one, or one that is as good? Why?
_____
_____

How many New Riders books do you own? _____

What are your favorite computer books? _____
_____

What other titles would you like to see us develop? _____
_____

Any comments for us? _____
_____
_____
_____

Solaris Essential Reference, 0-7357-0023-0

Fold here and tape to mail

- -

New Riders Publishing
201 W. 103rd St.
Indianapolis, IN 46290

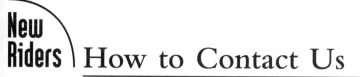

How to Contact Us

Visit Our Web Site

www.newriders.com

On our Web site, you'll find information about our other books, authors, tables of contents, indexes, and book errata. You can also place orders for books through our Web site.

Email Us

Contact us at this address:
newriders@mcp.com

- If you have comments or questions about this book
- To report errors that you have found in this book
- If you have a book proposal to submit or are interested in writing for New Riders
- If you would like to have an author kit sent to you
- If you are an expert in a computer topic or technology and are interested in being a technical editor who reviews manuscripts for technical accuracy

newriders-sales@mcp.com

- To find a distributor in your area, please contact our international department at the address above.

newriders-pr@mcp.com

- For instructors from educational institutions who wish to preview New Riders books for classroom use. Email should include your name, title, school, department, address, phone number, office days/hours, text in use, and enrollment in the body of your text along with your request for desk/examination copies and/or additional information.

Write to Us

New Riders Publishing
201 W. 103rd St.
Indianapolis, IN 46290-1097

Call Us

Toll-free (800) 571-5840 + 9 + 4557
If outside U.S. (317) 581-3500. Ask for New Riders.

Fax Us

(317) 581-4663

Colophon

The image on the cover of this book is a Landsat image of Easton, Pennsylvania, taken circa 1997.

Easton was founded in 1752 by Thomas Penn, the lesser-known son of William Penn. William was perhaps best known as the urban planner of Philadelphia (the plan from which, not coincidentally, Easton was designed) and one of the few colonial Americans to treat native Americans with some degree of respect. In 1682, he enacted the "Great Treaty," a land for goods quid pro quo, with the Leni Lenape (Delaware) tribe in the town of Shackamaxon.

After its founding, Easton thrived and played a role in the Industrial Revolution. Nestled between the Delaware and Lehigh rivers, it was part of an important trade route, and eventually became a stopping ground for five major railways to and from New York and Philadelphia. As a result of this economic prosperity, Easton's commerce and culture began to flourish. Continuing this trend, Lafayette College was organized in Easton by its citizens in 1826, led by James Madison Porter and Joel Jones. It eventually received its charter and opened in 1832, specializing in military science, literature, and general science.

One of the most colorful additions to the Easton landscape was the Crayola Crayon Factory, which was founded in 1900. Originally interested in making slate pencils, the founding company, Binney & Smith, settled in Easton because of the ready access to slate (for slate pencils, *natch*) and power from the Bushkill Creek. Crayola eventually manufactured the colorful drawing sticks now known as Crayons, which are made from paraffin wax and colored pigments. Some interesting Crayola factoids: The name is derived from the French word "craie" and the English "oleaginous," truncated to "ole" (translated literally: oily chalk). 100 billion Crayola crayons have been produced over the years, which is about five million crayons *a day*! Amazingly, the smell of Crayola crayons ranked 18th in a worldwide survey of the most recognized smells. The only colors that have ever changed names, (or are scheduled to do so) are "Prussian Blue," which changed to "Midnight Blue," "Flesh," which changed to "Peach," and "Indian Red," which has not been renamed yet.

One of the spookiest sites in Easton would have to be the State Theater, which is supposed to house *Fred the Ghost*. This paranormal presence is said to be the ghost of J. Fred Osterstock, manager of the theater from 1936-1965. Although there is no empirical evidence for the existence of Fred, several ostensibly reliable witnesses have had the luck to gander the ghost, including members of the State Board of Directors and the historian Ken Klabunde.

Today, Easton is home to nearly 27,000 industrious inhabitants. The local police station receives nearly 21,000 service calls per year. When 27 is added to 21, it equals 48, a popular number of crayons found in a specific type of Crayola box, rivaled only by the 64 box with built-in sharpener. Numerological coincidence, or cosmic concurrence? The editors withhold judgment, awaiting more evidence.

John P. Mulligan, author of this book and renowned environmental engineer, lives and works in the Easton area.